BEYOND DOUBT

BEYOND DOUBT

Four Steps to Inner Peace

John J. Murphy

Library of Congress Control Number:		2009908977
ISBN:	Hardcover	978-1-4415-7058-1
	Softcover	978-1-4415-7057-4

To order additional copies of this book, contact:
Xlibris Corporation
1-888-795-4274
www.Xlibris.com
Orders@Xlibris.com
67832

CONTENTS

For peace on earth . . .
as it is in heaven

BOOKS BY
JOHN J. MURPHY

- *Reinvent Yourself: A Lesson in Personal Leadership*

- *Agent of Change: Leading a Cultural Revolution*

- *Pulling Together: The Power of Teamwork*

- *The Eight Disciplines: An Enticing Look into Your Personality*

- *Get a Real Life: A Lesson in Personal Empowerment*

- *Think Change: Adapt and Thrive, or Fall Behind*

- *Do More with Less: 21 Principles for Thinking Lean*

COMMENTS ON OTHER BOOKS

'There is a book I want you to read. As a syndicated columnist, I regularly get books sent to me, often several in a week. I look through them all, hoping to find a gem . . . and I have! It's John Murphy's *Reinvent Yourself.* What I admired most about the book is that it captured the relationship between work, personality and family. It is heartwarming and soulful and a good read.'

—Dale Dauten, Author *The Max Strategy*
Excerpt from the Chicago Tribune, syndicated by King Features

'The ability to change and adapt in today's world is critical to success. John Murphy's book, *Agent of Change* does an outstanding job detailing how we can lead people and organizations through change. I highly recommend this book to anyone desiring to improve their personal leadership skills.'

—Peter F. Secchia
Chairman, Universal Forest Products
Former Ambassador to Italy

'Reengineering isn't just about changing corporate systems and structures. It's about getting people to feel more autonomy and ownership in what they do. That's what I like about John Murphy's book, *Reinvent Yourself*. It focuses on change at the personal level. I highly recommend it.'

—Dr. Denis Waitley
Author, *The Psychology of Winning*

'If you want a strong, positive 'jump start' to your professional and personal lives, then John Murphy's books, *Agent of Change* and *Reinvent Yourself* are must reads! These books penetrate right to the core of principle-centered leadership and proactive change management. I highly recommend both of them to anyone looking to lead a more fulfilling life. John Murphy is a winner—and so are his books!'

—Ed Robertson, Brig. General USAF (Ret.)
Communications Officer, Desert Storm

'You must and will change. *Agent of Change* will help you do it properly.'

—Richard M. DeVos
Co-founder Amway Corporation
Author, *Compassionate Capitalism*

'I can't help but tell you how much I enjoyed *Reinvent Yourself.* The easy story telling style made it a real page turner. I think we all need to continually reinvent ourselves, . . . so thanks for giving us the outline to do just that. Keep up the good work. You are making a difference.'

—Rocky Bleier
Four-Time Super Bowl Champion

'*Agent of Change* is a book for anyone who is trying to change things, whether it be at work, home, or in the community. Let John Murphy be your guide through the mine fields that accompany any change effort.'

—Dr. Ken Blanchard
Co-Author, *The One Minute Manager*

'. . . Finally, a concept that realistically addresses the communication and motivational problems in everyday business. *Pulling Together* is a definite must for today's manager who wants to lead effectively and break through the paradigms that stand in the way of real progress.'

—Ted Gedra
Executive Vice President, Wolverine Footware Group

'John Murphy's *Agent of Change* applies to *all* organizations. He speaks directly to all those seeking to create high performance work environments. I highly recommend!'

—Michael J. Brennan
Former President, Heart of West Michigan United Way

'*The Eight Disciplines* is a fresh and unique introduction to the Myers-Briggs Type Indicator concepts, particularly valuable because it teaches through applications.'

—Ken Taber, Outplacement Counselor

'Unusual, inspiring, thought-provoking. *Reinvent Yourself* is a wonderful story with implications for both the home and the work place. Send me twenty copies right away so my staff can read it.'

—Bert Bleke, Superintendent (retired)
Grand Rapids Public School System

'*Agent of Change* is a remarkable book. While the subject matter is about change through management systems, the principles involved transcend its setting. The ideas John Murphy presents speak as powerfully to interpersonal relationships and volunteer organizations such as the Church as to becoming an agent of change within a business environment. I read it eagerly and have passed on copies to my friends. I recommend it highly.'

—Rev. Gary T. Haller, First Church

ACKNOWLEDGMENTS

The first person I acknowledge and thank for this book is you. You are the reason I wrote the book. Thank you for starting and completing the circle.

I thank God for giving us a circle to work with, the circle of life. It is here that we learn and grow and share what we know. I thank the Holy Spirit for channeling these insights to me and through me so that you can learn what I am learning and co-create new circles with others. I thank Jesus, Buddha, Krishna and Lao Tzu for your timeless words of wisdom and demonstrations of love.

I thank the many mystics, spiritual masters and enlightened souls who have illuminated my path. Through your courageous, generous and empowering work, you lead by example. Thank you for caring and for sharing. Thank you for being a teacher of teachers. I give a special thanks to the Dalai Lama, Dr. Deepak Chopra, Dr. David Hawkins, Dr. Brian Weiss, Sri Siva, Barefoot Doctor, Lama Surya Das, Nikko Hansen, Sylvia Boorstein, Swami Veda Bharati, Swami Chidanand Saraswati, Dr. Alberto Villoldo, Sequoya Trueblood, Linda Fitch, Baba Harihar Ramji,

Thich Nhat Hanh, Sharon Salzberg, Byran Katie, Gregg Braden, Lee Carroll, Kryon, Gary Renard, Dr. Lee Pulos, Eckhart Tolle, Dr. Ravindra Kumar, Dr. Wayne Dyer, Thomas Moore, Gary Zukav, Dr. Denis Waitley, Dr. Ken Blanchard, Marianne Williamson, Robert Grant, Dr. Michael Cutler, Vic Conant, Gary Chappell, Dr. Helen Schucman and Dr. Bill Thetford. I also want to acknowledge the Institute of Noetic Sciences (IONS), the Association for Research and Enlightenment (ARE) and the prophetic readings of Edgar Cayce.

I thank the entire team at Xlibris Corporation for your help in bringing this book to market. I give a special thanks to Dona Gruet, Lana Hadormio, Sam Daniels, Maryjoe Summers and Philip Sarthou.

I thank my mother and father, my siblings and all of my extended family for being exactly who you are and for teaching me so much.

I thank my wife and children. I am forever grateful to share life with you and to learn from our many blessings together. Thank you for choosing me. I love you beyond doubt.

'Where are you going this time, Daddy?'

'To China,' replied the teacher.

'Do you speak Chinese?'

'I know two words.'

The child looked puzzled. 'Do you know who you will be teaching?'

The mystic smiled. 'No. Not yet. I will know soon enough.'

The child paused to think about this. The stillness offered comfort. 'Are you afraid?'

The teacher leaned forward and looked deep into his daughter's sparkling, inquisitive eyes. 'No, sweetheart. I am not afraid. You see, there is no fear in the nature of my work.'

FOREWORD

'There is no need to be afraid.'—Jesus

In the East, there is a saying, 'Think deep and act small.' Such is the life of a spiritual mystic, a 'teacher of teachers' who gently guides seekers of Truth so that they may pass the lessons on to others, deepening their own understanding along the way. Such is the reason for this book.

I am a teacher of teachers, a spiritual mystic serving as a business consultant. The nature of my work is love. It is with genuine love and compassion that I offer this book, a guide on how to transcend doubt and experience the joy of inner peace and equanimity. This is an adventure without distance, a constancy of purpose. It is daily grace. We are all of God and our shared purpose is to return to God, our natural state of mind. This is not a matter of choice. It is simply a matter of time. God is very patient. His will is being done, even if we temporarily deny it.

We all have enormous potential beyond the world of doubt but we also have tendencies that limit us, often without conscious awareness. This book teaches how to identify, understand and remove the self-imposed barriers impeding true progress. These obstacles are usually found in the mind, bound as thoughts of fear and disbelief, limiting growth and keeping people trapped in a state of illusion and quiet discontent. In corporate circles, we refer to this transformation as profound culture change, a pulling together of people to let go of resistance, eliminate disbelief and awaken to new possibilities. Through this innovative, corrective and healing process, extraordinary gains are manifested and shared, elevating participants to heights they never knew existed.

To fully accept my mission, I have had to learn to overcome my own doubts. When I started my consulting practice in 1988, I was surrounded by disbelief. At the time, I was unemployed, overloaded with debt, and my wife and I were expecting our second child. Our house was in disrepair and my car would shake violently at any speed over 55 mph. I needed work and income, not to mention insurance and health benefits. That is when the idea of consulting called to me. It also called to my two original business partners who accepted the call for about six months and then hung up the phone. This left me facing a rather large mountain to climb with very little gear, or so I thought. I was eager to offer my insight and help to the world, but it seemed a daunting task to start from below 'see' level. Why not just play it safe and find another management job? Why risk everything pursuing a life of uncertainty?

These questions continued to follow me for years to come. Do I play it safe, or do I risk it all? Do I live my life as a settler or as a pioneer? The first question is fear-based and defensive. It suggests that there is something to worry about, something to lose. This question leads to hesitation and resistance, as if judgments have already been made in the mind. The second question is spiritual. It suggests that the only real loss in life is forfeiting the gain that exists on the other side of courage. This loss can weigh heavy on the soul because, sooner or later, it carries with it the burden of wonder, guilt, grief and despair. Spirit asks why *not* go with the flow of life? Why not pursue your purpose? Why resist that which is natural? Why not be free?

These questions so intrigued me that in addition to teaching business 'best practices,' I began learning and sharing spiritual best practices as well. This meant digging deep, really deep, into the underlying barriers to inspirational leadership, authentic empowerment and high performance teamwork. Soon many of my clients—with gentle guidance—began discovering certain fundamental truths and synergistic results for themselves. Now, it was their own experience that guided them, not some theoretical model based on blind faith. This is what a spiritual mystic does. He inspires deep, fundamental, transformational change, the type of change that cannot easily be undone. He leads people to solutions without giving them answers. He helps people change their minds about their minds. He inspires people to realize the objective of their objectives. He teaches people to *see* the world differently by giving them something new and motivating to experience. And he leaves behind 'teachers' to share this message of authentic, unconditional love, grace, equanimity and genuine empowerment.

To affect this kind of change one must go far beyond communicating with words, pictures, tones and body language. These variables help, and in fact are necessary in day to day affairs, but transformational change requires illumination, love and awakening at the soul level. It is in fact an energy transfer, a miraculous means of release from suffering, doubt and fear. At our core level, we are free, joyful, unfettered spirits, eager to fully participate in life on this planet but anchored by a fearful ego mind that resists uncertainty. The inspiring leader helps people see things differently, altering some of their deepest assumptions, memes, values and beliefs, thereby hoisting the anchor of fear and liberating the spirit. He changes more than business processes, superficial habits and lagging indicators. He inspires mind change, freeing the soul and the physical body to ascend to new heights. This results in a shared sense of confidence, joy and genuine motivation. You feel this when certain people seem to 'light up the room.'

On a recent project in France, I was given a useful example. Some of the team members were quite candid with me on day one of the five day assignment. "Why should we try this again now? We tried this technique 15 years ago and it didn't work. Why does this particular process improvement matter so much? We have extra capacity and we are the top performing site in the global corporation." I smiled to myself. This team needed *context*, understanding and light. Without illumination, the team and the *content* would be lost in the dark and the project would be sure to follow. Worse, a subconscious form of resistance and doubt would remain, making future changes even more difficult. What this team needed was a miracle, a natural correction, an altering of perception, an expression of love, a means to let flow what is meant to flow. We went to work, finding ways to unite and work as one collective mind. Within five days, the transformed team found and tested a way to improve the process over 100%. During a five-hour test on day four, several of the most senior managers on site, including the site director, came to witness the inspiring event. The change in human energy from Monday to Thursday was indeed miraculous. On Friday, it was like working with an entirely new team.

In retrospect, the experience of teaching thousands of people from dozens of different countries and cultures has taught me more than I ever expected. As a result, I find that I am the student as much as I am the teacher. In fact, I am both, always, day and night, at work and at home. Even when I sleep, I am channeling insights from the collective mind and discovering ways to share the lessons. The key is to open the mind, suspend judgment and honestly listen to the voice of Truth, the divine force that gives us life. The same is true for you. You are a teacher and a student. You teach what you *think*, always. The lessons are revealed in your feelings and in your behavior, a perfect reflection of the thoughts you hold in mind. Thus, you are not only teaching others by what you demonstrate but you are teaching yourself as well. Be conscious of this. Pay attention to the thoughts you hold in mind and remember that you have a divine guide, a higher Self or consciousness, who can help you discern Truth from falsehood. The purpose of this book is to help you facilitate this process in whatever situation you are in. It is written from my own personal experiences, blending modern day applications and ancient spiritual principles into a four-step, continuous model, the Ring of Peace. My intent is to give you a tool that is easy to remember, simple to understand and miraculous in effect.

You will get the most out of this book and the Ring of Peace if you commit to four things:

1. *Open* your mind. Suspend all judgment—at least temporarily. Do not resist or close your mind, even if you do not believe what you are reading. You do not need to believe in Truth to experience Truth. Let your own results guide you.

2. If your ego objects (which it will), let it know you are aware of it. Say to yourself, "Ego, I know that's you. Be silent." Remember, you are *not* your ego, even though your ego wants you to think you are. You have power over your ego.

3. Try the model and the suggested exercises. Be *willing* to experiment. Let yourself be free to experience the power and grace of enlightenment.

4. Focus your efforts *internally*, not externally. Find your own equanimity and peace of mind first. The world cannot be at peace if you are not at peace.

Notice that I am not asking you to believe in my words or have 'faith' in this model. It is not a religion or dogma or cult. The enlightenment process is purely experiential. The only way to truly *know* it works is to experience the results personally. You must feel the light for yourself. As a spiritual mystic, I have come to realize that life is one great experiment, best understood through discovery. We really have no idea what is going to happen day to day—although we sometimes think we do (i.e. ego). Thus, being a student with an open and inquisitive mind is a good first step. Perhaps this is why you are reading this book. A little help from a trusted source can shine light on any soul. Books, CDs, DVDs, lectures and mentors have certainly helped me immensely on my journey, giving me invaluable companionship, insight and support. I have committed countless hours to researching and applying united spiritual counsel—ranging from the Bible to the Tao Te Ching to the Buddha to the Lost Gospels to the original teachings of Jesus and *A Course in Miracles* to modern day lamas, shamans, gurus and mystics—to everyday life. This is in addition to staying current with business best practices, which is what I happen to use as my vehicle for application and delivery.

During this period, I have learned to see the world as one, without separation, and with only one true need, the need for authentic awareness, forgiveness and atonement. We are all one. We are all teachers and students, givers and receivers, brothers and sisters in Spirit, capable of bringing enlightenment and salvation to the world—if we just *allow* it. Embrace and honor this God-given privilege. Give it *your* will. Open the door to your own awakening and inner peace. As a role model and teacher, remember that you *demonstrate* what you think throughout each day. The lessons appear in the way you walk, the way you talk, the way you greet people, the way you respond to good and bad news, and the way you say goodbye. Your students, including yourself, are learning from the expression on your face, the movements of your body, the messages in your eyes, the tone of your voice, the images you hold in mind and the energy field that surrounds you. Notice this when you come in contact with certain animals, perhaps a pet. They pick up very quickly on your energy, which translates instantaneously into your physical look, mood and movement. This means that you must be very conscious and vigilant of every thought that occupies your mind. There are no idle thoughts. You demonstrate and teach what you think and what you think becomes your perception of reality—even if it is not true. You see what you think you see.

When I first started teaching formal classes, I stumbled upon an ancient eastern phrase which translates into, "When the *student* is ready, the teacher will appear." The obvious wisdom in this simple statement is something I have experienced time and time again. It always helps to have a student with an open and willing mind. More recently, I have discovered an even deeper reality, a truth that speaks right to the heart of the spiritual teacher. The reality is this, "When the *teacher* is ready, the students will appear." Your readiness is the key to unlocking the doors that lead to your enlightenment and the positive impact you have on others. Be ready. Learn to listen to your higher Self and acknowledge the grace and wisdom that flow within you. Your light, essence and inner peace will attract and inspire others to take note and follow your lead. Prepare yourself and the students will come. Be awake and the lessons will appear. There is peace on earth. Nirvana is here and now. Heaven is not a place. It is a state of mind. There is no time and distance to the kingdom of God. It abides in you. It abides in all of us. Recognize this and others will too.

— John Murphy

Let Be
  Let Go
Let See
  Let Flow

CHAPTER ONE

The Ring of Peace

'My teaching is like a finger pointing to the moon.
Do not mistake the finger for the moon.'—Buddha

Most people are conditioned to think linearly. We learn to read linearly. We are taught to write linearly. We are trained to count linearly. We plan our days linearly. We view and manage time linearly. Everything seems to move in one direction, in a sequence. People organize their week, eat their meals, set their alarm clocks, count birthdays, plan for retirement, all with a somewhat linear mindset. The past is behind us, the future is in front of us and we move in one direction. To the linear mind, the four-step model would look like this:

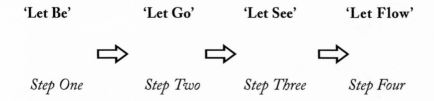

'Let Be'   **'Let Go'**   **'Let See'**   **'Let Flow'**

Step One   *Step Two*   *Step Three*   *Step Four*

Fortunately, the four-step model is *not* arranged this way. This is fortunate because if it was, it would not hold up in a non-linear universe, the realm of Spirit. People would find 'Step One' so challenging and overwhelming, relatively few people would get past it. It would be like trying fifteen different diet plans or exercise routines without sustainable success. We might be able to 'let be' for eleven seconds or so, and then the ego mind would take us back to the races again. It's time to pick up the kids at school. I have a report due first thing in the morning. I can't stop thinking about what so-and-so said yesterday. My boss really bums me out. I can't wait to go on vacation next month. Chatter. Chatter. Chatter.

A life of inner peace is not about following a historic recipe or a linear roadmap to some *future* state of bliss. And it is not about reliving the past or carrying the past into the future, which is what the ego mind is programmed to do. It is about *releasing* the constraints in the ego mind that limit immediate success. This is why I am going to explain the model beginning with what the linear thinker sees as 'Step Four' and work backwards. I can just hear a few skeptics now. 'Wait a tick. You're going in the wrong direction! You skipped the first three steps.' I love this reaction because intuitively, I know that Spirit, your higher Self, will help you 'see' differently, one of the actual steps in the model, when you 'experience' differently. In other words, we will replace the common "I will believe it when I see it" paradigm with its inverse, "I will see it when I believe it." When this happens, a slight shift will take place in your perception and you will experience a moment of enlightenment. What better way to learn and alter perception than by experiencing what is written instantaneously? You can help facilitate this process yourself by taking a moment now to contemplate a time in your life when you experienced pure bliss or the natural state of 'flow.' From here, we can examine the factors that enabled this peaceful state of mind with a more complete appreciation for how it is accomplished and why it matters. This *context* will help us with the *content*.

So think now about a time in your life when you were in flow. You may have been singing, dancing, gardening, designing, writing, drawing, painting, counseling, nursing, operating, lecturing, playing a sport, playing the drums, giving blood, helping a neighbor, meditating, making love or any number of activities where Spirit was shining through. In other words, you were inspired in the moment and you were inspiring to anyone in your presence. You were here and now and you were *in-Spirit*. In this state, you were breathing with a sense of calm and poise, you were at ease yet highly effective, and you were experiencing a sense of communion, timelessness and synchronicity. You were in flow. There was no fear or doubt in your mind. There was no feeling of shame or guilt or anger haunting you. There were no thoughts of yesterday or tomorrow, good or bad, right or wrong, us and them. Your body, mind and spirit were in perfect harmony and balance. You were operating as one with the oneness of the world around you. You did not ache or worry. You did not have an agenda. You were not harboring any hard feelings. You were perfectly immune to grief, temptation, disease, distress, pain and suffering. This was more than a proud moment. This was a moment of pure bliss, a flash of enlightenment.

We have all experienced glimpses of enlightenment. Perhaps it was a sudden 'aha,' when our mind's light went on or a moment when we were awakened with a sudden insight or revelation. These moments usually come and go quickly and often appear when people least expect them or are 'playing' in some way, like a child. During these moments, we have 'let go' (Step Two) of our thoughts, feelings, inhibitions, resistance, mental filters, underlying assumptions, memes, beliefs and boundaries. We are in a mode of release, stillness and discovery, genuinely open to the natural flow of life. As a result of letting go, we 'see' (Step Three) with a new sense of vision, even if only momentarily. The problem most people have is that these moments come and go so quickly, even while we are sleeping, that they pass by with little notice. It is more often an exception when a musician, writer or poet awakens suddenly in the night and actually writes down a brilliant insight. Just imagine what life would be like if you could accelerate the frequency and duration of these moments—and remember them!

In addition to explaining the four steps 'backwards,' I will also introduce the model as a ring, so there is no definitive end in mind. This challenges another common human paradigm, yet is consistent with spiritual Truth. At the spiritual level, we have no beginning and no end and we are anything but linear. We just are. We existed long before we entered our bodies and we will exist long after. Intuitively, we know this, but on the conscious level we are tempted to question it, perhaps even resist it, causing great conflict in the mind and fueling the fire of fear. Later on, we will examine these self-imposed limitations.

Let Flow (4)

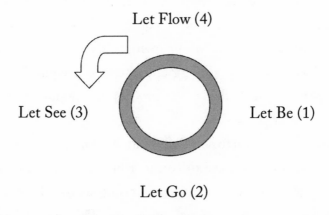

Let See (3)   Let Be (1)

Let Go (2)

Keep in mind, the purpose of the model and the overall objective of this book is to help you reach a more continuous state of inner peace and a heightened sense of spiritual awareness in the now, the on-going 'Let Be' step. This means feeling at peace in any situation at any time no matter what. To reach this level of imperturbability, we need to have some appreciation for the dynamics and interdependencies of the four steps and their relationships with one another. These steps are not independent (even though I will initially explain them this way), they are not linear, and there is no point at which we stop and consider the journey complete. This is a spiritual practice, not a destination. If we do not understand these dynamics, we may not accept the discipline and right-mindedness required of each interdependent step. For example, if we have a tendency to first look 'outside' ourselves for solutions—to the boss, to the minister, to the government, to the doctors, to the scientists, to the schools, to family, to friends, etc.—any step that suggests the answers are actually *within* us will make no sense at all. Who is comfortable 'letting things be' if in our own minds we are experiencing a sense of lack or conflict? Who is comfortable 'letting things go' when in our own minds we think we need them? Keep in mind, skipping any one step is equivalent with skipping them all. It delays the process of enlightenment and denies us inner peace.

It is also important to note that the model is multi-dimensional, just like we are. We have to consider not just one trip around the Ring of Peace, but many, each raising us to a higher level of consciousness and spiritual awareness. This symbolizes the Kundalini, or spiritual energy within each one of us, rising from the base of our spine toward our crown chakra as we become more enlightened. Thus, the process is on-going, requiring time and depth, so we acknowledge these dimensions as we make our ascension. For now, consider the following image.

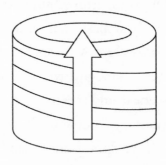

With this image in mind, note that each time we apply the Ring of Peace and ascend to a heightened sense of being, the now is perceived differently, even if the physical characteristics appear to be the same to the human eye. When we are in flow, we are free of mind clutter. As a result, we see more clearly through the mental debris that surrounds us. Without the burdens of grief, apathy, shame, guilt, desire, fear, doubt, anger, anxiety, jealousy, drama, and pride weighing us down, we feel 'lighter' and more awake to the fascinating world surrounding us. In this more awakened state, we perform at higher levels. We think more clearly. We sense and intuit more effectively. We feel more connected and engaged. We are more focused and aligned with the things that matter most in life. We experience more synchronicities and natural coincidences just by directing our intentions. This is what the process of enlightenment is all about. It is about cleansing oneself of all the clutter the ego mind thinks is important and freeing ourselves to achieve far more of our true potential. The Buddha described enlightenment as the release from suffering. I would add that it is the *acceptance* of joy, our natural state. To accomplish this, we must acknowledge any pain we have in the present and let it go. Denial and resistance and clinging to illusions will not set us free. We have to get in touch with the natural flow of life and the love surrounding us, seeing only the innocence and beauty of God's creations. Enlightenment is about letting go of the limitations of our *own* minds, the illusions we think are real, and joining wills with the one true Will that matters.

Now consider for a moment a life without flow. What is this like? Is it tiring trying to keep up with the rapid pace of the world racing by? Is it frustrating separating the important from the unimportant in a mind that doesn't know the difference? Is it exhausting bouncing between past and future like a ping pong match? Do the possible sometimes seem impossible? Does there appear to be a shortage of time or energy or money, which is merely a form of energy (i.e. currency)? Do other people tend to be annoying? Do people frequently get upset? Do people sometimes think that in order to win someone else has to lose? What does it feel like when life appears to be spinning out of control? Does it make people feel like clinging tighter to what exists now, even if it is weighing them down? Does it seem like a life of inner peace is nothing but a distant dream, an idealistic impossibility?

Now consider why people might think this. Could it be that some people do not *see* themselves living in a state of flow? And why would we not see this? Is it possible that we might be blinded by our own filters, our own paradigms? And why would these mental barriers exist? Why would we not *let go* of them? Is it possible that our current state is so cluttered with debris and negative self-talk that we cling to the only thing we do know, a life of sacrifice and misery? Do people even go so far as finding ways to rationalize sacrifices, calling them gifts to God, as if God wants us to suffer? If this sounds at all familiar, it is because it is a very common self-defeating, vicious circle. It is like running on a treadmill to nowhere, seeking ways to justify the means. Sooner or later, we get tired and become frustrated, perhaps even angry. We appreciate family and friends who understand, but some who appear to understand may actually compound the problem. Misery always has loved company. We begin to think it is a test of will or bad karma. Nothing we do seems to work. It is the same pattern, over and over again. The current state is bad, so we justify our own experience by projecting our subconscious defeat outward onto the world around us, giving us evidence that we are right. Everywhere we look, something is wrong. Just look at the news and some of the delusional shows on television. The government is corrupt. The environment is in trouble. The schools are deficient. Prices are too high. There is too much traffic. Certain people irritate us. Even our vacation turns up several things to complain about. So we cling tighter, seeing less and less of the beauty that coexists with the pain. We see only the half empty glass, never enough to cheer about for long. And the more people see the world this way, the more the world reflects back this unfortunate perspective. The collective ego mind, our combined interpretation, manifests these perceptions of defeat into physical evidence. We experience what we think we see.

It took me several years to break out of this vicious circle myself. Looking back, which I rarely do anymore, I recall some of the challenges I experienced playing football. This may not seem like the most relevant example, but for me football was a real passion when I was in high school and the lessons I learned have transcended time. I loved so many different elements of the game, the strategic play-calling, the tactical execution, the teamwork, the diversity, the timing, the discipline, the fitness, the pressure, the leadership development, the energy and the spirit. Of course, as with any sport, there is always adversity to overcome. In order to win, we have to learn how to get over a loss. For me, the most significant 'losses' came off the field. Two in particular were difficult to overcome. The first was a diagnosed hernia two weeks prior to my sophomore season. I was competing for the starting quarterback position and this news essentially benched me for the entire season, requiring six days in the hospital and eight weeks of recovery without physical strain. I cried for hours. This was a set-back during a critical development year that would be tough to put behind me—or so I thought.

The second incident came two years later, the summer preceding my senior year. This was an especially exciting time because we had just won the state championship my junior year and I was elected by my teammates to be a captain for our upcoming season. I was training hard every day and looking forward to a great season. In addition to daily conditioning, a friend and I were running a small lawn-mowing business. We had a very heavy workload on one particular day, the day before I was to go on vacation with my family. One of our customers asked me if I would mow some tall grass in her backyard to make room for a party she was planning. I said no problem. I was wrong. An hour later, I was in the emergency room with a severely damaged foot, my football dreams once again imploding. Six days of hospitalization and ten hours of surgery later, I was benched from football, this time for life according to the surgeon. The cycle seemed to have repeated itself.

As a mystic, one understands that there are no coincidences. Everything happens for a reason. While I was in the hospital, feeling a bit down, my mother gave me a book that my grandfather had sent. It was a book about courage, and it featured a story about Rocky Bleier. Rocky was a four-time Super Bowl winner with the Pittsburgh Steelers who overcame very serious foot and leg injuries suffered in Vietnam. He was originally drafted by the Pittsburgh Steelers from the University of Notre Dame, but he ended up serving in Vietnam before ever playing a down in the NFL. Following his injury, he was given the same advice I had been given. Give up. Let it go. Find something else to do with your life. I blazed through the Rocky Bleier story with anguish and anticipation. It spoke to me. Rocky had been in a situation very similar to the one I was in, much worse in fact, and he did what the doctors said he could not do. He overcame doubt. I remember feeling something in my heart that day that modern medicine could not explain. My foot would heal because my mind would heal. Spirit would see to that. This was the lesson I needed to learn. I needed to accept what is (let be), release any negative thoughts and doubts (let go), see the situation differently (let see) and be healed (let flow). Twenty years later, after the release of my book, *Reinvent Yourself*, I had the privilege of introducing Rocky Bleier at a large public seminar on motivation and success. I shared my story with him, thanking him for the profound effect he had on me, and I also shared *our* story with the audience that day. I would never have gone on to play football at Notre Dame without Rocky's inspiration and we may never have met without this serendipitous event. There are no coincidences.

Exercise:

Take a moment now to contemplate several different times in your life when you were in flow. What was your body doing? What was your mind thinking—if anything? How long did the feeling of elevated consciousness last? What barriers or obstacles did you have to overcome to reach this state? Why do you remember these particular moments over so many others?

CHAPTER TWO

Let Flow

'Stand before it, there is no beginning.
Follow it and there is no end.
Stay with the Tao, Move with the present.'—Lao Tzu

According to the ancient Tao, which literally translates into 'the Way' or the 'the Great Current,' we are born to flow. It is our natural state. This is not something we have to try to do. It just happens, like grass growing green, if we *let* it. There is a force, beyond us all, that keeps all things moving. Even our planet is hurling through space at over 65,000 mph and spinning on its axis at over 1,000 mph. There is no need to hold meetings or develop strategic plans to make this happen. It just does. What seems to be standing still is in continuous motion. Trees, rocks, mountains, ice, the human body, all are changing from one instant to the next, vibrating at various speeds. The atoms that make up the physical universe are in constant motion, and within each of these atoms is predominantly empty space. To put this into perspective, imagine an atom the size of a large football stadium. Now imagine the proton and neutron within this atom being about the size of a grain of salt. The electron spinning about the atom is even smaller. This is like looking up into the sky at night and contrasting the stars with space itself. The world we see is mostly empty space, pure consciousness, flowing at incredible speeds and responding to projections of the mind. Our bodies behave in the same way. Dr. Deepak Chopra writes in his book *Quantum Healing* that if you want to know what you were thinking three to four years ago, look at your body today. If you want to know what you are thinking today, look at your body in three to four years. Our thoughts, both conscious and unconscious, manifest into our perceived reality. The human body is in constant motion, over fifty trillion cells flowing continuously, without effort.

This does not mean that flow equals perpetual bliss. On the contrary, the Tao speaks clearly about the *yin* and *yang* of life, the downs and the ups, the perfect balance and harmony of the universe. These positive and negative forces (not good and bad, but simply opposite, even though people may *interpret* them as good and bad) are necessary in order for all things to work as intended. They are like the positive and negative terminals on a battery. Neither one is good or bad, but they are both necessary in order to generate current and power. We live in a perfect yin yang current. The grass appears to die, or go dormant, in the winter (yin) and is reborn in the spring (yang). We get hungry, eat, and feel full. We get tired, sleep, and feel rested. We buy a car or a house and it starts to show its blemishes. We make money. We lose money. We breathe in. We breathe out. We annihilate our foot with a lawn mower. We run through the tunnel at Notre Dame Stadium faster than we were prior to the accident. We make mistakes. We learn from them. Everything we experience has its natural ups and downs, its perfect life balance, if we *let* it. The trouble is, many people get overly discouraged during the yin moments and overjoyed during the yang moments and they interfere with their own inner peace by unconsciously setting their minds against it. As a result, they do not live with a sense of grace and peaceful flow. Life to the fearful mind is more like a white water rafting excursion, exhilarating from time to time but worrisome. Hold on tight! Who knows what is going to be around the next bend?

In order to live in a more sustainable state of inner peace and grace, we have to understand and accept our true essence. We have to understand flow and the life force behind it. We cannot live in flow if we hold onto fear, and we cannot release fear without understanding its origin. This means we must appreciate the cause and effect nature of the universe and the power of our own minds. Inner peace and flow are effects, caused by a higher power. We do not cause them because they already exist. They always have. On a collective, spiritual level, flow and the state of pure peaceful consciousness are already timeless and complete. All we need to do is tap into this level by removing the self-imposed barriers and limitations that stand in the way. This is like opening a faucet. Once the tap is open, the water flows. The tap does not cause the water to flow. On the contrary, the tap *prevents* the water from flowing, much like the mind prevents peace from reaching us due to our own fear. In life, we are in charge of the tap, which represents the power of our mind. We are in charge of removing the barriers to our own ascension because we are in charge of changing our own minds. No one else can do this for us. Jesus states in *A Course in Miracles*, that he cannot interfere with the law of cause and effect, the most fundamental law of the universe because doing so would violate our free will and the lessons we are here on this planet to learn. This is why each step in the four-step model begins with the word 'Let.' We must *allow* ourselves to flow by taking responsibility for the thoughts that we hold in mind.

This understanding has been a revelation for me. I grew up repeating an 'I am not worthy' mantra every Sunday and hearing that sacrifice and suffering were necessary steps to reach heaven. I learned that God was to be feared and that the Last Judgment would be like going to a grand courtroom in the sky. My image of St. Peter was that of a 'bouncer' at the gates of heaven, searching the Akashic Records for permission to enter. Never mind that little of this made much sense to a curious, intuitive kid. It was proclaimed as the Word and was not to be doubted. Thus, I found myself developing a 'consciousness' of poverty, pain and fear, a mindset that took me years to release. Add to this the fact that I was born on Friday the 13th with an ego like a steel trap and you can just imagine what my early years were like. I was in and out of the hospital so many times by the age of seventeen my mother considered putting a doctor on retainer. This pattern of 'bad luck' then followed me into college and my early years of employment, like a karmic cycle repeating itself over and over. It would have been easy for the ego mind to find ways to justify that I was somehow a victim in a world of evil, but my deeper 'Self' could not accept this. I had to wonder. Was it possible that I was manifesting my own pain and suffering by what I was projecting from my own subconscious mind? And if this is true, what might one create with a change in mind.

In the Bible, there is reference to Adam falling into a deep sleep after the separation, the fall from grace. Prior to the separation, everything was in a state of flow and bliss. There was nothing to fear and nothing to hide. Everything was in perfect harmony. Spiritually, we were all one with God. What I find interesting is that nowhere after falling into his deep slumber is there anything written about Adam 'waking up.' Does this mean that we are all still asleep to the perfect grace and inner peace that abides within us? Are we blind to the divinity of God running through us? Could the Garden of Eden be right in front of us, hidden by a veil called ignorance and ego?

In the Buddhist tradition, the 'way' is essentially found by waking up and recognizing four noble truths. In fact, the word Buddha literally means *Awake*. So what does it mean to be awake? Could it mean that we see the world differently, as the Buddha and the great bodhisattvas do? Could it mean that we see through the drama and theater of everyday life with the knowledge and wisdom of certainty? The Four Noble Truths provide further insight:

1. Life is difficult and sometimes hard to bear; there is suffering (Dukkha)
2. Life is difficult because of attachment and craving, there is a cause of suffering (Tanha)
3. The possibility of enlightenment and well-being exists for everyone; there is a way to end suffering (Nirvana)
4. The Way to liberation and enlightenment is through the Eightfold Path, meaning with Right View, Right Intention, Right Speech, Right Action, Right Livelihood, Right Effort, Right Mindfulness, Right Concentration (see table at end of chapter)

These ancient noble truths remind us that there is a cause and effect relationship between what we experience in life and what we choose in life. These truths also remind us that there is a way out of pain and suffering, a way 'home' to inner peace, but we must learn to choose differently. We must learn to let go to let flow. This is ultimately the reason we are here on earth. We must learn to take ownership for our choices and exercise our free will wisely. This is our mission: to find our way home. Again, this is why Jesus says that he cannot interfere with our free will and the natural cause and effect principle of the universe. It would violate our reason for being here. He has set an example by showing us the way home, but he cannot take our responsibility away from us without violating the most fundamental law of the universe.

The Buddhist practice also speaks of three deadly sins or kleshas. These are ignorance, attachment and aversion. Ignorance essentially means 'not knowing' the Truth, or not right mindedness. Attachments and aversions are both forms of desire, stemming from ignorance and causing a great deal of suffering. In other words, if we hold in mind thoughts of desire or lack, we automatically trigger a feeling of stress and dis-ease in our own consciousness. Without vigilance, these feelings of dis-ease can easily manifest into perceived mental and physical disease, evidence of that which we hold in mind. Some refer to this as the 'Law of Attraction', except that we are attracting the lack rather than the object of desire. In other words, lack is the equivalent of not having. So if we hold in mind the thought of lack, we will actually hold this lack (not having) in place. The object of our desire will continue to elude us. To use the law of attraction wisely, we must hold in mind the thought of having, not lacking, even if we do not yet have the object of our intent. There is a similar dynamic for aversions, desires we wish not to have. Examples of aversions might include illnesses, injuries, failures, embarrassments, poor grades, divorces, layoffs and hostilities. In universal terms, aversions translate into fear and if we dwell on fear it will manifest into perceived reality. We will actually attract that which we wish to avoid. The universe does not understand the negative. It only understands what we hold in mind. One often meets suffering on the path taken to avoid it.

In today's world, the word ignorance is considered a rather harsh criticism. After all, who wants to admit that they are ignorant? On the other hand, I find ignorance to be the most common root cause to problems and undesirable effects among people. We just don't know what we don't know, and it is very difficult to admit that we do not know what we are doing when we actually think we do, especially if we are in a leadership role. As a result, many people find themselves dealing with the same basic symptoms (effects) over and over again because they resist accepting the true root cause, their own ignorance and misperception.

Since people often think reality is what *they* perceive, rather than Truth itself, it is no wonder that the world is filled with so much fear and conflict. This is a difficult concept for many people to understand because it is common to think of oneself as a body, relying on the human senses to direct the mind. We hear statements like 'perception is reality' and 'I will believe it when I see it'. The ego mind tells us to accept what our human eyes see as the truth. This is deceiving. Perception is not reality because perception is of the body (visible) and reality is of God (invisible). Perception and reality cannot coexist in one mind. If we know God's Truth with certainty, we have no need for perception. Thus, perception only exists in the absence of knowledge and Truth, the absence of God. It tells us what to believe in when we do not actually know God's Truth with certainty. Going one step further, the only way to truly know is to be. One cannot know a tiger without being a tiger. We can only perceive a tiger and imagine what it is like. Thus to know God's Truth means we must be God's Truth. We must be in communion with our spiritual essence and the divine light giving us life. Our Spirit knows God's Truth because it is God's Truth—within each and every one of us, even if the ego denies it. Herein rests the origin of fear and doubt in the human being, both stemming from a mind that is confused, divided and in conflict. The ego is the source of this confusion. The ego denies the Truth of God within us, our own spiritual nature. The ego tries to convince us that the mind responds to the body when in fact the exact opposite is true. The body is neutral. The mind is the key to inner peace, which is then extended to others through a healthy body. Change your mind and you change the world around you.

True knowledge reaches far beyond facts and scientific analysis and superficial conflict in the material world. Where there is knowledge, there is no conflict because there is no perception, no judgment and no ignorance. This is nirvana, a state of mind without doubt. Here knowledge is connected with spiritual Truth which transcends intellect, science, time, position and matter. Spiritual Truth has no opposite. There is spiritual Truth, which the Holy Spirit recognizes, and there is the absence of Truth, which the Holy Spirit does not recognize. In other words, the Holy Spirit only responds to Truth—not the ego's perception of truth. This is why it is so important to guard your thoughts. The Holy Spirit is listening. This is also why the 'I am' affirmations are so powerful and effective. It is the language of the Holy Spirit. It is the language of the universe. When you say to yourself I am forgiving, I am compassionate, I am joyful, I am thankful, the universe responds in kind. It understands your intent. The same is true when you *feel* a desired state in the present. For example, when the Native Americans performed spiritual rituals like the rain dance, they actually felt rain in their mind's eye as a call to the universe. They did not pray *for* rain. They visualized rain in the now. This was not a message of lack; rather it was a message of having and being, a message of affluence and abundance. However, if you make statements like I am not afraid, I am not worried or I am not stressed, the universe will interpret this as "I am afraid, I am worried and I am stressed" and you will actually attract that which you wish to avoid. It is as if the word 'not' does not exist in the universal field of consciousness or in the mind of God. This is also true for prayer. If you pray *for* something, it reminds the universe that you do not have it, thus keeping you in a perpetual state of lack and desire.

Think of Truth as light. There is light and there is the absence of light, which we call darkness. The only way out of darkness is with a light. The light always diminishes the darkness. Feel the light in the now and you shall witness it. See the light in others and others will see it in you. Say to yourself, and to the universe, I am the light. I am Spirit. I am illuminating and free. Do not ask God to take away your darkness. He does not recognize it nor does He acknowledge it because He did not create it. We must remove our own perceptions of darkness because we created them in our own minds. God gave us the light a long time ago. We must let it shine through. Remove the blinders from your own mind's eye.

Love is another Truth. There is no opposite to love, only an absence or denial of love which results in fear and the disruption of flow. Fear exists when we are not aligned with universal Truth, either consciously or subconsciously. It is not God that we should fear. Fear is not an attribute of God. It is our own misinterpretation of the Truth, leaving us in a self-imposed state of darkness and doubt. To align with Truth, we must learn to see God's essence in one another and we cannot see this perfect Creation without letting go of our ego and directing our own divine light. Flow is a state of mind called heaven. It is a return to the perfect state of spiritual awareness where we all began. It is our true home, no matter where we are physically.

When we carefully and objectively examine the barriers to flow, we find ourselves staring straight into a mirror. We cannot achieve and sustain flow if any of the following conditions are present:

- We see ourselves or others in doubt; we do not really think a life of peace is possible; we hold thoughts like 'I am stupid' or 'I am not worthy' or 'I cannot do that' or 'It is impossible' or 'So and so is an idiot.'
- We see ourselves or others in fear; we do not trust God or 'the way;' we hold thoughts like 'I am afraid' or 'I do not know what to do' or 'So and so is weak.'
- We see ourselves or others as separate individuals, disconnected from the whole; we hold thoughts like 'I am alone' or 'I hate' or 'I do not trust anyone' or 'So and so is selfish.'
- We see flow as an external gift of some kind; we hold thoughts like 'I wish for' or 'I am a victim' or 'I have no choice' or 'So and so is the problem.'

Notice that each of these conditions indicates that how we see people in the world, including ourselves is essential to our own peace of mind. Recognize that if we see any negative in someone else, it is an admission that this negative exists in all of us because we are all part of the same oneness with God. And since God did not create anything negative, that which we see as bad is not real. It is not Truth. It is just an illusion of the ego mind. However, in acknowledging that it exists, the ego prevents us from ascending to higher consciousness. It binds us to a world of drama and conflict, often without our awareness of the limits we have accepted. Therefore, to 'Let Flow' on a reasonably consistent basis, we have to allow ourselves to see the world differently, beginning with ourselves and the people around us. We have to learn to see the Truth in others and in ourselves.

Exercise:

Take a moment now to contemplate how you view yourself in the world. Pay close attention to the internal messages you send your mind and body. Honestly, how would you complete the 'I am' affirmations? Write at least nine 'I am' affirmations. How do these statements make you feel? Are they positive and freeing, or negative and limiting? Be perfectly honest with yourself. Do you sense any hesitation or doubt? Where is this doubt coming from? Do you know with certainty? Now consider how you view other people. Do you see anyone in a negative way? To what extent do you have grievances, enemies or hostilities? Does anyone annoy you? Why? Do you have a tendency to criticize and judge others? What thoughts do you hold in mind about others? What do these thoughts tell you about yourself?

The 8-Fold Path—'The Middle Way'

1. Right View   See things as they are

2. Right Intentions   Be compassionate

3. Right Speech   Speak the Truth

4. Right Action   Demonstrate love

5. Right Livelihood   Make love visible with work

6. Right Effort   Be attentive, focused, passionate

7. Right Mindfulness   Be aware

8. Right Concentration   Be still; Enjoy meditation

Chapter Three

Let See

'Every kingdom divided against itself is brought to desolation;
Every house divided against itself shall not stand.'—Jesus

How long has it been since you held a negative thought and responded in a critical way? Think carefully. Consider all situations: a traffic jam, a slow computer, an unfriendly neighbor, a demeaning boss, a loss of money, an excessive bill, an interruption, a headache, a defective purchase, a stubbed toe, a challenging child. Do you find that you experience pain and anger frequently? Do certain people and situations annoy you? Are you someone who gets agitated and stressed often?

Now stop and imagine a life of honest, genuine peace, deep stillness, boundless joy and imperturbability in *any* situation. Think about how people would treat one another if we all tapped into this God given right. Seem impossible? What an outrageous concept, some might say. Such a life could not possibly exist in today's world. Centuries, millennia in fact, prove that the world is in a state of chaos. Wars exist all around us. Poverty is abundant. Crime rears its ugly head from Wall Street to Main Street. Violence is witnessed even at peace rallies and in church parking lots. People pray and ask for forgiveness and then return to patterns of impatience, anger, greed, doubt and disbelief. In this world, we have to protect ourselves, defend ourselves, and stand vigilant at all times. Suffering, pain and death cast very long, dark shadows.

Now consider who or what might respond in this way? Where are these reactions and voices coming from? Who is it that insists that a life of joy, abundance and peace is impossible? What is this force of resistance and what is so convincing about it that people accept such deceit? Is it possible that our own inner 'programming' has a virus? Could people be hearing and seeing life through clouded filters? What if the human race is being deceived by a most trusted source—the human ego mind?

Next question: Do people even know with certainty who—or what—they are? After all, if we are not actually who we think we are, our own mind could be deceiving us. Our entire perspective of the world and our participation in it could be an illusion. Ridiculous, some might say. This sounds absurd. Hostility and violence exist all around us. I have seen it with my own eyes and heard it with my own ears. Just turn on the daily news. The world I see and hear and feel day after day is not one of peace. It is one of pain and illness and distress. Heaven, if there is one, is somewhere else. It is certainly not here.

If you find yourself feeling or expressing any of these doubts, any of this resistance, you are not alone. In fact, your reaction is quite common. You are among the multitudes of people suffering because they are being deceived—at the subconscious level—about what they really are. They are suffering because they know of no alternative to suffering. They see themselves as a physical body or if not as a body, as a component of the mind, the ego, governing the body. So when the eyes 'see' something or the ears 'hear' something, the body responds as the ego mind suggests. Remember something, a corpse has ears and eyes but hears and sees nothing. So when we look in a mirror, it is the ego mind telling people what to see and it is the ego thoughts telling people how to feel about it. If the mind informs us that we are a temporary being defined by diminishing, at-risk physical characteristics, this information can be frightening, often at the subconscious level. Many people are not even aware that they are afraid. The mirror is reflecting pure fiction and the ego is reveling in the drama. Why are more people not at peace? The answer to this question lies in the ego mind itself, the fear within.

Jesus once said that every house divided against itself shall not stand. Recognize that these words are not just about countries and governments and businesses and families. They are about you and your own conflicted mind. You cannot be at peace if you listen to a mind of fear. And the world cannot be at peace if you are not at peace.

This raises several important questions:

1. What exactly is the ego mind?
2. Why is the ego mind afraid?
3. If I am not my body or my ego mind, who or what am I?
4. How do I learn to *see* the world differently?

What exactly is the ego mind?

The ego is the part of the mind that believes in separation. It is our animal instinct, a human characteristic designed for survival. It was given to us not by God, but by our collective rejection of God. As a result, it is what makes us feel apart, naked and vulnerable. The ego is the reason we tend to search for answers outside of ourselves, because the ego tends to deny any responsibility for our problems. It can't possibly be my fault, says the ego. I had nothing to do with it. The ego may even try to convince you that you have no ego, coaxing you into thinking that you are a humble, gentle and unique soul and that someone else's ego is the problem.

Do not be fooled by the ego. When Jesus said 'deliver us from evil,' he was referring to the ego and the separation that pulled us apart from God and from one another. Keep in mind, God recognizes no evil, just as He recognizes no ego. He recognizes only that which He created which is pure and innocent perfection. The concept of evil is a human creation, dictated by the ego. Beyond ego, there is no conflict and without conflict there is peace of mind, just as God intended. We suffer because the ego is ignorant of the Truth and it serves as our own internal barrier to God. We cannot reach God through the ego. This is the great test we all face while here on earth and it is this mission that the great spiritual masters have all embraced.

When I was growing up and first getting started in business, I was directed consciously and subconsciously by my ego. I was of an ego consciousness, deceived into thinking this was my true identity. During these years, my ego would have me think that I was an

'A' student, a gifted athlete, a man with certain physical features and characteristics, a creative entrepreneur, a loving husband, a caring father, an author, a consultant, a world traveler, a specific personality type, a successful businessman. These descriptions may sound good to the ego, which peaks at pride, but my ego could have just as easily tried to persuade me into identifying with the many failures I have experienced. In other words, the ego is equally responsible for convincing someone they are lacking in some way, despite any successes. It is the ego who says, "What you really need is a bigger house or a better car. You would do well to go back to school, earn another degree or achieve some unique title." The ego feeds on conflict and drama and superficial measurements of success. It indulges in life just as much when you are feeling miserable as when you are feeling accomplished. Even at its peak level of pride, it is the ego that wants to fight over some image of separation, be it school rivalries, government politics, religious beliefs or national differences. Wherever there is a flag flying or a coat of arms hanging, there is an ego thriving on separation.

Christians refer to the 'way' as salvation. It is ultimately accomplished through the atonement, a principle leading us all back to our conscious unity with God, or at-one-ment. We are saved when we finally see ourselves as one, as Jesus did, in Christ. The Christ is the oneness of us all beyond the ego. It is the Son-ship. It is the way. It is the divine nature we all share. It is the perfection within each one of us, pure and innocent, as created by God. True forgiveness then is an altering of perception, a different way of seeing a situation, where there is no evaluation, no ego, no judgment and no condemnation. It is right-mindedness. It is seeing past the ignorance and foolishness of the ego. When Jesus said, "Father, forgive them for they know not what they do," he was not judging. He was teaching. He was transcending ego and appealing to God for correction, not punishment. Jesus was showing us the way.

Judgment is a key characteristic of the ego mind. You will know your ego is attempting to take charge whenever you hear yourself or feel yourself judging other people, circumstances or things. It can be as simple as 'I don't like algebra' or as vengeful as 'I hate Mr. Jones.' These projections of the ego stir conflict in your mind and body. They manifest anger, hostility and deep subconscious feelings of suffering and grief. We would do well to remember that our judgments do no harm to anyone but ourselves so if we choose to hold on to such interpretations we are the ones who suffer. As Jesus said, 'Can anxious thought add a single day to your life?' When we judge, we simply reinforce the fear of being judged. When we attack, we remind ourselves of our own vulnerability to attack. When we criticize, we add guilt, lack and a sense of scarcity to our own subconscious mind. In reality, there is no separation. We are one with all that we judge, attack or criticize so when we hold onto negative thoughts and perceptions we experience negative results—often hidden from us in the unconscious mind and revealed later in time. This is also why I urge you to suspend any ego judgment while practicing the Ring of Peace. It will be your own ego that pushes back, seeking ways to protect itself from spiritual Truth. This is a very typical defensive and a logical move projected from fear. Just remember, you have power over the ego.

Why is the ego mind afraid?

The ego mind is afraid because it sees itself, like the body, as temporary. Any feelings of vulnerability we hold are not characteristic of Spirit. They are misperceptions of the ego. In fact, Spirit would have us know that real life does not even begin until *after* we have transcended fear and doubt. In other words, the ego's definition of life and Spirit's definition of life are completely different. The ego tries to convince us that life is bound from physical birth to physical death. Spirit knows with certainty that we exist before and after the body and that the body only serves as a temporary learning vessel while we are here. The ego seeks to have us feel ashamed, guilty, and angry about misgivings in the past and lust for gain in the future. The ego is not content in the here and now, which is why it is always pulling the mind forward into the future or back into the past. Spirit knows with certainty that neither the future nor the past are real, so the ego's definition of life is delusional. This is why the ego is afraid. It feels constantly threatened, knowing it is temporary and disconnected from God's eternal Truth. This is why the ego would have people fear God rather than itself. Some external force must be to blame. Admitting otherwise, without some hidden agenda, is beyond the ego's animalistic comprehension. Spirit being an extension of God knows there is nothing to fear. The life of Spirit—your true life—is not temporary. True life begins when fear ends.

Given the ego is of a temporary nature, like the body, and is not created by God it is limited to a life of perception and judgment. It is not capable of true knowledge. This means that it may perceive rightly or wrongly, but it cannot *know* God's Truth. It is separate from Spirit, without contact. Thus, it has little choice but to fear perceived pain and seek perceived pleasure. Since it is an instrument of perception, not knowledge, it must constantly choose what it thinks is best. And since it is born of separation and fear, it will always choose what it thinks is best for itself—independent of everyone else, including the holistic, spiritual you. This thought system, a foundation authored by humankind, not by God, triggers feelings such as:

- 'I feel worried. How am I going to pay the utility bill?'
- 'I feel bored. Let's *do* something fun.'
- 'I feel angry. My boss is not fair.'
- 'I don't like this place. Let's *go* somewhere else.'
- 'I feel upset. I should be making more money.'
- 'I feel depressed. Maybe I should see a doctor and get some medication.'
- 'I feel ashamed. I said something to my father I shouldn't have said.'
- 'I feel happy. I got an A on my report card.'
- 'I feel sad. My dog died.'
- 'I feel victorious. My team won the game.'
- 'I feel afraid. My retirement savings has been diminished.'
- 'I feel guilty. I should have done what my mother asked.'
- 'I feel lost. I do not know who to trust.'

Notice that with each of these feelings, there is an external attachment (or perhaps aversion), a clinging to some material interest. This is where the ego seeks pleasure and associates pain—outside of itself! It could be a connection to another physical body, a form of approval or a desire for control. These attachments to external things—be it a person, a pet, a position or a paycheck—trigger fear because they are temporary and at risk. The ego revels in this drama, its own version of yin and yang, but it is a far cry from spiritual stillness and inner peace.

If I am not my body or my ego mind, who or what am I?

We are Spirit. The mind and the body are extensions of Spirit. In other words, there is so much more to people than meets the physical eye. At our highest level, we are connected through the Holy Spirit with God and the oneness of the universe. We are the Son-ship of God, brothers and sisters in Spirit, united in perfection. We are consciousness itself, divine in origin and living without boundaries and sin. This is the inner peace that abides deep within each one of us, often buried beneath years of misperception and wrong-minded programming. It is our true sense of security and unbounded freedom. This is the light of God and heaven within, our true natural state. This is what Jesus saw in others, the Christ, and what others eventually saw in him.

Our challenge is this. When we arrive in our bodies we carry with us certain karmic lessons or imprints from the past with new challenges to overcome—all necessary for us to ascend to our true natural state and finally return home 'debt-free.' Add to our core reason for being here all of the human expectations, rules and boundaries imposed on us by parents, family, friends, schools, governments, employers, the environment and our own ego, it is a wonder anyone can remember who they truly are. From the day we are born, we are told 'do this' and 'do not do that.' This is an apple and that is a chair. This is cold and that is hot. Believe this and do not believe that. Go here and do not go there. Say this but do not say that. These human values, beliefs, expectations and boundaries do not define who we are, but often the ego thinks they do. This is why it is so important to the ego that you attend a certain school or pursue a specific career or reach a certain level of income and power. These measures fit in well with a 'self' defined by the human ego, but they mean very little to your true, capital S 'Self,' the divine Spirit within. Your true Self is much more interested in acts of love and generosity, without attachment or greed. Your true Self seeks a life of acceptance and joy, not judgment and grief. Your Spirit within thrives when you do what you do because you truly love it and find pleasure in giving to others. This is life beyond fear and doubt. It is a life of affluence and abundance, where the more you give the more you receive. Thus, you may appear on the surface to have great prosperity and wealth, but it is your deep connection with the totality of the universe that keeps you feeling rewarded and motivated. After all, Spirit knows that you cannot actually have anything of value unless you are willing and able to give it away. You cannot have true love if you do not offer it. You cannot have forgiveness if you do not forgive others. You cannot have peace without giving it away. When it comes to what is truly real and of God, there is no scarcity in the universe. Your Spirit thrives when you accept this universal principle.

Think for a moment about why you do whatever it is you do for a living. What motivates you to get up every day and do what you do? Is it your purpose or is it the paycheck? Is it your passion or is it the position? Is it an expression of love or a countermeasure to fear? Is it your heart making the call or is it your head? These questions go beyond identifying your calling. They ask who is making the call. Is your work spiritual or egocentric? This distinction can make all the difference.

At a recent spiritual workshop, a participant told me he mowed grass at a golf course for a living. This gentleman was well over 70 years of age and spoke very highly of his relationship with God while mowing grass. He spoke of certain vantage points on the golf course where he liked to stop his tractor and watch the rising sun, listen to the songbirds and be in communion with God. This was not a job to him. It was a joy. This was not an ego-calling. It was spiritual freedom. The fact that he collected a paycheck for doing something he loved was pure gravy.

How do I learn to see the world differently?

Put simply, flow is a state of mind—a way of seeing and being of higher consciousness. It is an ability to get in touch with the beauty, the harmony and the innocence that surrounds us each and every day. It is an ability to see planet Earth as the perfect learning ground for humankind, a place where karmic lessons far beyond our ego comprehension must be accepted, learned and appreciated. Granted, there are plenty of problems to focus on and complain about, but this is the drama the ego has had us dwelling on for millennia to keep us from experiencing our own true state of grace. Remember, if we are not at peace internally, the world can never be at peace. The temptation to focus externally, an ancient ego trick, has kept humankind searching in all the wrong places for sustainable solutions that exist only within us.

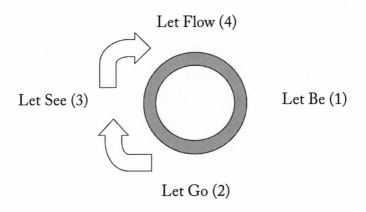

To achieve and ultimately sustain flow, we have to alter the way we see the world. It is not the world we have to change, but our minds about the world. To experience flow, we have to see flow. We have to know flow. We have to expect flow. Alternatively, if life is not flowing well for us now, it is because we are not seeing right. We are misinterpreting or perceiving wrongly, a common ego malfunction. This has little to do with our physical eyes and everything to do with our mind's eye. In *A Course in Miracles*, Jesus states quite clearly that seeing with the vision of Christ and seeing with the body's eyes are exact opposites. One cannot see what the other sees. It would be like seeing light and dark at the same time. To 'Let See,' people must learn to *let go*. This means removing the blindfolds that cover the mind's eye. The ego is blind of reality and does not even know it. The ego sees only the temporary, and never the Truth. The ego is so easily influenced by the mass media, politicians, pundits, educators, business leaders, bosses, friends and family—many of whom have no concept of enlightenment and inner peace. We live in a world of egos trying to convince egos of falsities and misperceptions. Trouble is the ego is an instrument of perception rather than knowledge and therefore it does not know the difference between Truth and falsehood. Thus, many in the human race are blindfolded and deceived by the trusted ego mind.

So how do we learn to see differently? What is it we have to 'let go' of in order to see with the vision of Christ? The answer lies in the mind. A change in mind results in a change in vision and a change in manifestation. The key is to find the right leverage points to release. Letting go of these 'root, root causes' frees people of any unconscious guilt buried away in their subconscious mind. Take note that these leverage points exist internally, in the mind, and nowhere else. If people perceive themselves as victims, they cannot be free. They will wait and wait and wait for some external force to free us all and it will not happen. Ownership and empowerment reside within us. The 'second coming' abides within us. We must exercise our own free will to free our will. This begins in the here and now, the perpetual moment of Truth. It is in the 'Let Be' step that we truly begin our ascension, which

I will speak to in Chapter 5. This is the 'as is' state, the 'what we reap' moment. It is what is and it cannot be changed. When enlightened, it is a moment to be thankful for, a moment of love and joy and inner peace, even if the outcome is not what the ego desires. With the light of God shining through, every moment is perfect when you see beyond doubt.

At higher levels of consciousness, one realizes that anything temporary is not real because it was not created by God. The only thing that is actually real is that which is created by God, or co-created with God. These realities are perfect in nature, abundant and eternal. There is no beginning and no end. They are beyond perception, time and space, and without physical properties. In other words, the 'real' is invisible to the human eye and the unreal is visible. So what is it we actually see? And what is it that we attach ourselves to that leads us into a state of fear? Do we attach ourselves to certain people, places and things? Do we then spend years worrying about 'losing' these people, places and things—all of which are temporary and unreal to begin with? Do we associate ourselves with certain values and interpretations that mean nothing to Spirit? Do our ego fears trap us into feelings of loss, desperation and paranoia? Even with the death of a loved one, do we experience more of a loss or a gain? Clearly, at the ego level we mourn a loss to our physical and mental 'self.' On a higher level, however, our spiritual 'Self' rejoices in welcoming home a kindred soul.

In 2000, my father passed on and I must admit that at the time, my ego was hurt. I wanted to fight—and I wanted my father to fight—the cancer that was eating away at his body for eleven months. I didn't want to 'lose' my father and in some ways, this seemed like a great battle to me. We needed to batten down the hatches, prepare our defenses and go on the attack. We needed to find the right doctors, hospitals and medicines to take on this devastating adversary. It was us against the cancer and we were determined to win. Obviously, I was ignorant of Truth at the time and felt compelled to 'will' myself, my father and my family, against the great current of life. Being dominated by the ego-mind, I had little regard for the bigger picture, the spiritual context. This was a win or lose situation. It was us against it, victory or defeat—despite the reality that *any* outcome on the ego level would only be temporary. This was a battle of perception, not of knowledge. As a result, it was my ego that suffered. It was my ego that got caught up in the drama with my siblings, my mother, the doctors, the details. It was my ego that felt fear, grief, anger, loss and despair. From a spiritual perspective, I never did lose my father. I am closer to him today than I ever have been before. He visits me in my dreams. He sends me messages. He communicates with my wife and children. He is free. For this, I am thankful.

To many cultures, death is a beautiful passage. It is not something to fear or to fight, but to accept as a necessary step on our journey home. The ancient Mayan culture, for example, views the physical death of a body as a form of release, a transition to a higher realm. Shamans perform rituals facilitating this passage, closing the chakras at the appropriate time to free the luminous energy field from the body and ease the ascension. This is a very honorable milestone in life, like that of physical birth or reaching puberty, and it is viewed with joy, peace and spiritual understanding. That which the ego fears most is really a blessing in disguise.

Exercise:

Take a moment now to contemplate the things you tend to resist in life. Consider all aspects of your life. At a minimum, consider ideas, thoughts, feelings, temptations, people, places, activities, age, health, weather, events, commitments, investments, responsibilities, risks, values and beliefs. How many times per hour or per day do you find yourself resisting something? Why do you do this?

CHAPTER FOUR

Let Go

'The five colours blind the eye. The five tones deafen the ear.
The five flavours dull the taste. Racing and hunting madden the mind.
Precious things lead one astray.
Therefore, the sage is guided by what he feels and not by what he sees.
He lets go of that and chooses this.'—Lao Tzu

Working 'backwards' through the model, we see that flow is our natural state, our essence. It is the eternal state of the universe, whole and complete. It is the 'mind' of God, a field of luminous energy, a life giving force, a quantum hologram where each particle of light contains the image of the whole. This is where we are connected. This is where we are one, pure and innocent, beyond the human eye. When we get in touch with flow, we get in touch with our true nature, our innocence and perfection, the way God created us. In some practices, this flow is referred to as the Tao, the 'Way' or the 'Great Current.'

Other practices refer to the experience of flow as an 'awakening' or 'enlightenment.' It doesn't really matter what we call this natural state and it is only the ego that wishes to label, argue or debate it. It just is. It is our connection to God through the Holy Spirit. It is through the divine light within each one of us that we eliminate the dark shadows of ego and recognize Spirit, our true Self. We are more than a body and we are more than a mind. We are not bound to the ego 'self' and its limited perceptions and we are not temporary. We are Spirit and we are free.

The problem for many people is that they do not *feel* this freedom. As a result, they doubt it. That is to say, the ego doubts it. In fact, the ego fears spiritual freedom and urges people to be suspicious. Why? Because the ego is a mad idea — a tool — that wants us to believe that we are one in the same with it — temporary, bound and incomplete. It is a car that wants us to think we are the car. It is a hammer that wants us to think we are the hammer. It craves control, approval and security and feels forever threatened with or without these temporary illusions. It feels compelled to run your life, if you let it. The ego is in a no win situation and this is frightening. It senses its own limitations and ultimate demise. Keep in mind, we are not the tool. We are the *user* of the tool. We use the body and we use the ego mind, but they are only temporary components of our true Self. Do not lose sight of this. The body and the ego mind can serve people well as vessels for communion, but we are responsible for exercising free will and right choice. We can change our minds and the mind can heal the body, but to do this wisely, we need to be in touch with our higher Self and the best interests of the common good.

We must learn to see ourselves differently, as already whole and complete, and we must listen to only one voice, the voice of the Holy Spirit, our direct connection to God.

In order to see ourselves and the world we live in differently, we have to remove certain blindfolds. These blindfolds are not of a physical nature but rather of a mental and emotional nature. They are misperceptions of the ego, resulting in wrong-minded thinking. They prevent us from seeing Truth, leaving us feeling doubtful and confused. It is no wonder that so many people suffer from internal disturbance. They are not aware of the blindfolds binding them.

The 'Let See' phase requires examining two critical components to *feeling*. The first component is thought and the second is emotion. Together, these two factors manifest feeling. They also represent two rather significant blindfolds, factors we need to manage and potentially let go. Symbolically, consider this equation:

$$\text{Thought x Emotion = Feeling}$$

Every minute of every day, we are bombarded with thoughts. Think of thoughts like raindrops in a rainstorm. They just keep coming, filling our minds with constant chatter. Sometimes our thoughts are meaningful, but more often than not they are completely meaningless. This is especially true in the untrained mind that has not learned to disengage (perhaps through meditation or contemplation) from mind chatter. Many of these thoughts are of the past—which does not matter—while others are of the future—which does not matter now. In either case, they distract from the present moment, the only time that really does matter. We find ourselves living in the past or future, but missing the now. This is like taking an excess of photos or video at a birthday party and actually missing the party or obsessing on a future event that never comes. These are not bad ideas, just examples of how easy it is to miss the moment. This is also why so many people struggle with meditation. Meditation is the practice of disengaging from thought long enough to experience the stillness, grace and wisdom that exist between thought. Meditation is about *listening* to God. It is not about asking God for anything or praying to God with a list of petitions or an agenda of some kind. It is about looking into heaven from earth, witnessing the splendor and the glory of God that exists in the stillness. It is a form of release from all thought, allowing us to experience the vision of Christ and spiritual flow. It is about seeing through the veil that separates heaven and earth, a veil bestowed upon us by the ego when we were born into human form. There are numerous meditative techniques, several of which I use daily. Tap into the many resources available, including books, retreats, television, DVDs and CDs if you are interested. Just be sure to remember the spiritual reason for meditating, the objective of the objective, even if it is only for fifteen minutes a day. You will feel more awake and more aware throughout the entire day.

Looking specifically at the *thought* factor in the equation, note the following potential failure modes and the impact they can have on how you feel:

- Too many thoughts, leading to a feeling of being overwhelmed, no peace of mind
- Thoughts that are not true, leading to feelings of jealousy, despair, anger, etc.
- Thoughts that are irrelevant, leading to wasted time and inefficiency

Winston Churchill once said, 'The price of greatness is responsibility over each of your thoughts.' It is absolutely essential that we stand vigilant over our thoughts. We cannot stop thoughts from coming, and it is a mistake to try, but we can stand watch over the thoughts we choose to carry and those we elect to let go. This is the first blindfold we must remove, the unnecessary and misleading thoughts that occupy the mind. With this release comes a tremendous sense of freedom. Just stop and ask yourself from time to time, "How would I feel without this thought?"

The second factor in the equation is *emotion*. There are many different interpretations of this word, ranging from its Latin root, *emovere*, which means to disturb, to common 'feelings' such as shame, guilt, sorrow, grief, apathy, anger, jealousy, pride, love and joy. I will keep it simple, using only two emotions, love and fear. In reality, the Holy Spirit reminds us that there is only one true emotion. It is love, and there is no opposite to love. There is only the absence of love, decided by humankind and resulting in fear. Therefore, I will use fear as the alternative emotion to love. This emotional factor in the equation is a critical variable in determining the impact of the feeling. For example, if I hold a thought such as 'What if I lose my job?' and this thought is coupled with an emotion of fear, the resulting feeling will likely be anxiety, stress and (ego) self-protectionism. The idea of 'change' could even be somewhat paralyzing. However, this same thought coupled with true, spirited, unconditional love, springs forth a feeling of adventure and new beginnings. 'What if I lose my job? I will move on to something else, something better. It will be as it is meant to be.'

This example may sound a bit far-fetched, especially in a world riddled with unemployment. But the example is not far-fetched when one looks at it from beyond the fearful ego. Love in the context of the equation above is not a conditional love. It is not a love that rests upon a return love, or a quid pro quo exchange. It is pure love, without condition, without fear, everlasting and true. There is no opposite, so no matter what happens, Spirit continues on joyful and free. Someone with this perspective does not hold grudges, does not get down on himself and does not accept a gloomy outlook. He moves on. He lets go. He works with the flow, not against it. Truth is, someone with this perspective would not worry about losing his job in the first place (i.e. would not hold that thought or aversion), and as a result, probably would not lose the job. This is how powerful perspective and belief can be. It takes on two forms, thoughts and emotions, which when combined generate feeling which then manifests into perceived reality. Plug in any thought with any emotion and see what feeling you get. Or take any feeling you are having and trace it back to the thoughts you are holding in mind and the emotion you are using to fuel the thoughts. This may be one of the most profound exercises you ever do. You will learn that you do have control over your feelings.

There is another reason my example is not far-fetched. I live it. As an independent consultant, paid only when work is contracted and provided, I change jobs several times a year. Without fear, I am able to transcend this perceived pressure and constant uncertainty. I would be in a state of panic if I gave into my ego. This is why the nature of my work is love. With love, passion overcomes fear and certainty reigns. There is nothing to worry about.

Since there are literally billions of possible thoughts to mind, most of which are held in the unconscious mind, a useful technique in uncovering key, subconscious thoughts that block vision and flow is to examine tendencies. This includes any tendency you have to resist that which is natural. Examples here might include:

Tendency	Underlying Thoughts
• Resist aging	I am losing control, approval, identity, youth . . .
• Resist ideas	I am threatened, vulnerable, at risk . . .
• Resist certain people	I am jealous, angry, threatened, judgmental . . .
• Resist certain foods	I am allergic, weak, judgmental, risk averse . . .
• Resist exercising	I am lazy, afraid, embarrassed, have no time . . .
• Resist travel	I am fearful, biased, nervous, pessimistic . . .
• Resist something new	I am losing control, at risk, afraid to fail . . .
• Resist learning	I am stupid, not capable, arrogant . . .
• To feel angry	I am jealous, judgmental, pessimistic, afraid . . .
• To feel impatient	I have no time, under pressure, arrogant . . .
• To feel incomplete	I need someone else to be happy, complete . . .
• To feel shame	I am a sinner, guilty, wrong . . .

- To feel desire   I am lacking, weak, lustful, without . . .
- To feel afraid   I am in doubt, unsure, at risk, vulnerable . . .
- To feel defensive   I am being attacked, I need to protect myself, . . .
- To be in doubt   I am ego . . .

When we analyze any negative feelings people have, we find that they are harvested by a fearful ego mind. Feelings of jealousy, for example, are cultivated by thoughts of selfishness, control and distrust, and fueled by fear. Feelings of rage stem from thoughts of judgment, superiority and perceived mistreatment, and are energized by fear. Thus, the two most important 'blindfolds' people must manage vigilantly are thoughts and emotions. Choose carefully that which you hold in your mind and choose wisely that which you hold in your heart. Let go of all else. Let go of fear to begin with. Fear generates stress. You have nothing to fear. It is only your ego that would have you think otherwise. Let go of your ego thoughts. Why live in doubt? Let go of shame. You have no shame in the present. Let go of guilt. Spirit knows no guilt. Let go of grief. You need hold no grievances in the now. Let go of the past—all mistakes, grudges, hostilities, dislikes, unfortunate events. They mean nothing now. Let go of disbelief. Let go of the thoughts that stress you. Let go of the thoughts that agitate you. Let go of the negative self-talk. Let go of your pride. It is a barrier to greater joy. Let go of the causes to your own suffering. Recognize that what you hold in mind becomes your experience. This is the world of perception and judgment, the world of the ego mind. Let go of negative perceptions of yourself and of others. Let go and let God. Forgive and be forgiven.

Exercise:

Consider your current situation in life, including relationships, work, finances, health, family, location, attributes, limitations, spirituality and dreams. What annoys you? Why? What thoughts do you hold in mind to make you feel this way? How would you feel without holding these thoughts?

CHAPTER FIVE

Let Be

'Can you remain unmoving till the right action arises itself?'
—Tao Te Ching

One of the most common temptations of an intuitive change agent is to skip the 'Let Be' step. Who has time to stop and smell the roses? The current state just isn't good enough. We cannot accept the present. There are too many things going wrong. There is pain and suffering everywhere. We cannot sit still. We need to advance. We need to improve. The world calls for change. We need to do something now!

As a business consultant, I have seen this over and over again. My clients want improvement and they want it fast, especially during the yin, or down cycles. The mantra I hear every week is 'better, faster, lower cost!' Customers demand more. Shareholders demand more. Employees demand more. We cannot let up. We cannot let be. This often leads people to jump to solutions, perhaps solving one symptom while unintentionally creating several other problems. We see the same paradigms in health care, politics and religion. We overcorrect. We overcompensate. We overproduce. We over-regulate. We oversupply. In an effort to make life better, we complicate it. *We add when it would be wiser to subtract.* Thus, with one quick decision or judgment, not grounded in systemic reality, we cause several other undesirable effects. In time, this often results in a vicious circle and we find ourselves swimming in a manmade pool of yin yang far beyond human comprehension. We have inventory and clutter no one wants. We have laws that don't matter. We have people dying from prescribed medicines and unnecessary surgeries. We have people suffering in wars they do not want or understand. We spend money we do not have on things we do not need. We draw ego lines in the sand without spiritual understanding and we end up hurting ourselves and others.

The *Let Be* step challenges us to stop, to listen, to open our minds to the perfect balance and wisdom of the universe. With this step comes the understanding that there is no effect without a cause, and there is no problem without a solution. Everything in the universe is in perfect systemic balance. Everything is alright. This is the step where we learn to accept what is—right now—because within this step lies the wisdom that what is right now cannot be changed. It just is. Use this step to learn from it. Appreciate it. Be grateful. Love what is. Surrender the moment to God.

Of course, this can be hard to accept when your life feels like it is in a state of chaos. It is especially hard to appreciate the present moment if you have not yet practiced the 'cycle' of the

Ring of Peace a few times. In other words, if you have not yet awakened to the natural flow of the universe, the Tao, the yin and the yang of life, the God force, the Holy Spirit, the divine field—or whatever name you choose to give the energy field that connects us all—this may feel like a big step. After all, who has time to stop, to just be, when we are in a perceived crisis mode with deadlines to be met? How can one trust some invisible force when the writing on the wall says 'Act now?' This is again why I have presented the Ring of Peace backwards. To fully appreciate the power and grace in the Let Be step, we must see it in relation to the other steps and the bigger picture. We need context to fully understand the content of this very significant step.

To begin with, any time we see the present—the only time that really matters—as lacking in some way, we contribute to the cause of suffering. As the Buddha taught, there is suffering. No doubt about it. Few would deny this noble truth. However, there is also a cause for all suffering and the cause begins in the mind, the ego mind. This cause is usually associated with a feeling of lack, a desire of some kind, an attachment or an aversion. In other words, we are not at peace if we think (and thus feel) that we are missing something or are at risk of some kind. This could be anything from wanting to lose a few pounds to desiring a career change to worrying about a loved one. If the mind holds onto these feelings of lack and threat, the world cannot be at peace. Each day will haunt you, frighten you, and fill your mind with worry and doubt. From here, you will cling tighter, rather than release and let go, and as a result you will not see the glory and stillness of each moment throughout the day.

You will completely miss the perfect serenity and balance of life itself even though it is right in front of you. And because you will not see it, you will not flow with it. This is the message Jesus meant for us to hear, even as he was being nailed to the cross. If you choose not to learn to still your mind, acknowledge and release your ego thoughts and fears, you will not feel the light of God and experience the true meaning of life. You will be trapped, unknowingly holding some outside force accountable for your suffering, and praying to God (perhaps) for some miracle when the true miracle abides in your own heart, your altar of Spirit. You were given the right to live a life of peace and joy, despite the circumstances. Choose it.

Recently, my oldest daughter texted me a note expressing her anxiety over a problem she was facing. The problem was that her apartment lease was expiring and she was being forced to leave by the end of the month. She had already extended the lease to allow her extra time while her offer to buy a condominium was approved. Unfortunately, the offer on the condominium was tied up with a bank for an extended length of time (as in months) and she was now about to be without a place to live. In addition, the friend she was planning to share the condo with could wait no longer for a place to live, so she was planning to withdraw from the deal. Given my wife and I lived over 2,000 miles away, there was little we could do to physically accommodate her during this transition so she needed to find a solution in her local area. In short, my daughter feared being homeless for a period of time and her stress and anxiety were clearly evident in the note she wrote me. My response was simple. I asked her to take time immediately to close her eyes, concentrate on her breathing, still her thoughts, listen to her own heartbeat, feel her blood running through her body from fingertips to toes and then thank God for all she had. I urged her to do this for at least 10-20 minutes. In other words, I urged her to let be and let go. I asked her to be positive and accept whatever comes her way. A short time later, I received a 'thank you' text from her and a promise to do as I suggested. Later that night, I received a second note from her, this one telling me that she had been approved to 'rent' the condo, effective immediately, until the final sale went through. I am sure you can imagine the delight that came through with this note. Her problem had been solved, quickly and effectively, and the stress she was accepting earlier was meaningless.

It is important to note that prior to this 'letting go,' she had put many ideas and actions into motion. By no means is the letting go step intended as a form of apathy or carelessness. On the contrary, my daughter had set goals, followed through with action and put things in motion. In other words, she had things to let go of. She had set her intention, given it her attention and then let it go. This is how the cycle works. She had to 'be' focused and proactive and then trust in a higher power. It is from here that we 'see' with more wisdom and clarity and ultimately experience flow.

During this very same period, I had a very interesting conversation with my oldest son who was interning with me on an assignment in Scotland. He was aware of his older sister's note and predicament and he was interested in the advice I offered. We discussed the Ring of Peace model and he shared with me another simple and practical example. This one had to do with his classes at Michigan State University. He explained to me that he had set a goal of getting a 4.0 during his sophomore year. He went on to say that he then just 'let it go.' He studied hard and stayed focused, but he did not stress over it or create unnecessary pressure. This allowed him to see more clearly, relax and experience flow. And he was very pleased about getting his 4.0 grade point average. He manifested his intent without being attached to it.

These may seem like simple examples, but my intent is to show you how the model applies to a variety of different, potentially stressful situations. We start with the *Let Be* step and follow with *Let Go*. What follows is often perceived as miraculous. Here are a few practical suggestions on how we can apply this powerful and profound step toward enlightenment. Keep in mind as you practice these suggestions that each of them begins with the word 'Be,' not become. Thinking in terms of *being* is a significantly different state of mind than thinking in terms of *becoming*. When we let be, we remind ourselves of our true essence in the eternal now. When we think become, we distance ourselves from the now and reinforce a feeling of lack.

Be Still; Mind Your Breathing:

This may sound simplistic, but most people struggle being still. The mind is always racing, thinking unnecessary and distracting thoughts. As a result, we are often completely unaware of the eternal now. We push serenity into the future, away from us. Attending to our breathing is one of the most important things we can do to change this. It is a simple way of connecting with life itself. With each breath, we inhale Spirit and we exhale tension. Breathing is one of our most natural expressions of flow, or disruption of flow! Pay attention to your breathing. Take time each day to disengage your mind from thought and focus only on your breathing. Do not analyze it or judge it. Just feel it. Describe it. Attend to it. Let it cleanse you. Let it heal you.

Be Positive; Clarify Your Intent:

Your intent reflects your underlying emotion and sets direction for you throughout the day. Are your intentions positive or negative, light or dark, loving or fearful, Spirit or ego? Think carefully about the underlying intentions in the words you say, the feelings you experience and the things you do? Why do you say the things you say, feel the way you feel, and do the things you do? Examine and describe your intent. Clarify it. Look deep within yourself for any cause of suffering (e.g. fear, doubt, attachment, aversion, suspicion, control, approval, ego . . .). Do you really think you need to change the world, or perhaps change your mind about the world? Ask yourself. What is your intent? What is holding you back? What do you need to let go of?

Be Aware; Take Inventory:

Examine carefully who you are and what you have. Do not be fooled by the ego. Use the 'I am' and 'I have' affirmations to reinforce your understanding of yourself—your true spiritual

Self. Consider affirmations such I am Spirit, I am eternal, I am whole, I am complete, I am honest, I am above and beneath no one, I am healed, I am confident, I am accepting, I am joyful, I am abundant, I am loving, I am forgiving, I am flowing, I am affluent, I am one with God, I am accepting, I am free. I am at peace. These affirmations help awaken you to the Spirit within and manifest positive outcomes throughout the day.

Be Thankful:

Take time each day to give thanks for all that you are and all that you have. Do not pray *for* something, which is an expression of lack for some other time. Instead, thank God for what you already are and what you already have—in the now, even if you do not yet think it is true. Examples might include:

- Thank you God for giving me the wisdom and strength to endure the situation I am in.
- Thank you for healing me. By your light, I am healed.
- Thank you for the lessons I am learning from _____.
- Thank you for giving me the patience, compassion and love to get through this difficult time.
- Thank you for the tremendous opportunities I have each day to grow and prosper.
- Thank you for giving me my daily bread and for delivering me from ego.
- Thank you for allowing me to be a teacher of teachers, a messenger of God and one with the Holy Spirit

Be Present:

Notice how quickly your mind likes to wander and leap from one timeframe to another. Use meditation and contemplation techniques to discipline your mind, disengaging you from your thoughts and constant mind chatter. For simple meditation, close your eyes, listen to your breathing, focus attention on specific parts of your body (e.g. your right eye, the tip of your tongue, your heart, your toes, your solar plexus, your chakras, etc.) and tell them to relax. Listen for your own heart beat and feel your blood pulsate through your body. If you are hurting anywhere, focus attention on that part of your body, tell it to relax and allow the chi energy force running through your body to massage and heal the affected area. In time, move your attention to your 'third eye,' located between your eyebrows and corresponding with your pituitary gland. Pull your perspective back into the center of your head (what the Taoists call the 'Original Cave of Spirit') near your pineal gland and witness the extraordinary colors and visions that come to you. Stay in this present state for 15-30 minutes once a day to elevate your consciousness and presence. Think of it like a mind shower, to accompany any physical cleansing you do during the day.

For contemplation, choose a different affirmation, mantra or healing sound to hold in mind throughout each day, returning to it each hour to reconnect with the moment. This helps you focus your intention and attention on who you really are and what your mind and body are doing in the now. Be sure not to criticize or judge any affirmation or mantra. Just think it. Privately chant it.

Be it. Let it flow through you. For example, if you have a troubling commute to work each day, consider trying an affirmation like 'I am at peace no matter where and no matter what.' Allow this affirmation to help you find gentle laughter when you get cut off or compassion when you are being tailgated. Perhaps the next day you try an affirmation like "I love the time I have in my car to listen to classical music." It would probably be helpful to then experience the work of Mozart or Beethoven while you wind your way through traffic. Who knows? Within a month or two you might be listening to Tibetan chants, Vedic mantras or Taoist healing sounds, channeled and shared to bring you in closer touch with Spirit by releasing self-defeating ego thoughts and emotion.

Be Joyful; Smile and Laugh:

A sure sign of enlightenment and being in the moment is a genuine smile or gentle laugh. Remember, your natural state is one of joy. When you are free of all the ego clutter, rigidity, comparisons, competition, measurement, rationale, pride, worry, stress, doubt, grief and fear, you feel lighter, happier, more at ease. You see the humor in things. You see the balance, the beauty and the perfection. People who used to annoy you now amuse you—not in a negative, judgmental way but in a more understandable way. They are just doing what they are supposed to be doing. It is like they are playing a role in a movie. You may not like the character, but you know that beneath the character is someone different, a pure and innocent soul. It is like seeing the drama being played out from a totally different perspective, perhaps from 100,000 feet up! This person, *who you used to let annoy you*, is now just doing exactly what he or she is meant to be doing. You now see this purpose and you recognize the lesson within it, a lesson you are now thankful for. This soul helped your soul advance. You were meant to go through this.

Be Compassionate; Feel What You Feel Without Being Attached:

Many times when we are feeling down or out, we respond with resistance or attack. These are not welcome feelings, so we try to beat them away. Deep down at a spiritual level, we don't want to fight. We don't want to feel ashamed, or fearful, or lustful or angry. We deserve better than that. So we push back. And the more we push back, the more we strengthen these feelings. Keep in mind these feelings are generated by the ego—ego thoughts fueled by the emotion of fear. Thus, any attempt to combat, deny, resist, overcome or punish the ego will result in counterattack. In other words, we cannot defeat the ego with attack. The only defense against the ego is love. It is through love that we forgive and silence the ego. It is with love that we accept the atonement and are delivered from the ego. It is love that heals us. Try this the next time you feel guilty or sad or doubtful or angry. Let it be. Observe it without judgment, attachment or aversion. Learn from it. What is the internal cause to this effect? Do not blame it on anyone else. Blame is simply a projection of your own self-doubt and unconscious guilt. When you blame others you are subconsciously blaming yourself, generating even more unconscious guilt and fear. This is a vicious circle, a pattern keeping you trapped in negative tendencies. You cannot be angry without judgment. And you cannot judge without thought. What thoughts and tendencies are driving your anger? Find the cause and let it go.

Be Sensing:

One of the most important disciplines in the 'Let Be' step is to pay attention to your physical self, your body. Think of your body as a cathedral, housing the altar of Spirit, your heart. It is in your heart that your passion abides. If your cathedral is in need of repair, you need to know this. You need to be aware before the walls come crumbling down. The sun is shining bright, but if it is lost in dark clouds, you will not see or feel its radiance. How often do we meet people who are disheartened, dispirited and perhaps even 'broken-hearted,' only to see this weakened state of mind manifest into bodily distress? Use your senses to attend to your body and the environment you live in. Listen to yourself, your breathing, your heartbeat, your pulse. Taste the food and the drink you allow into your body. Chew the food slowly, acknowledging the communion between you. Savor the aroma, the texture and the nutritional value of each bite or sip you take. Pay attention to the facts about what it is you are accepting into your body and learn all that you can about the advantages and disadvantages of various combinations. Contemplate what Hippocrates, the ancient Greek physician said, 'Let food be thy medicine and thy medicine—food.' Beware of misleading marketing and useless—even dangerous—substances. Look at what you eat and what you do and learn from it.

Your senses are also extremely useful in keeping you aware and grounded in the eternal now. Be sure to smell the flowers when you see them. In fact, stop and plant some flowers from time to time. Get in touch with the earth. Listen to the birds chirping and the insects buzzing, or the running water of a stream or fountain. Observe the natural flow that is taking place all around you each and every moment of the day. The earth turns. The leaves on the trees rustle. The clouds roll by. The sun rises and sets, leaving glorious artwork in the sky for you to witness. People walk by. Conversations take place. The world is a beautiful stage in constant motion. Honor it with your presence. Begin right now. Take this moment to stop reading and dedicate the next five minutes to observing, feeling, smelling, listening to, and perhaps even tasting the world immediately around you. Do this as if you were in slow motion, attending deliberately to everything around you, one at a time.

Be Fit; Exercise Your Mind and Body:

One of the fastest ways to embrace the Ring of Peace is through exercise. What better way to let be, let go, let see and let flow? Through proper exercise we can get in closer touch with our breathing (especially if we are swimming), our body, our heart rate, and our mind. This is a wonderful way to release tension and stress, humble our egos and achieve flow—even if only temporarily. You also have many different forms of exercise to choose from, the most basic of which is probably walking. Taking a long walk, especially in a natural setting, is one of the easiest and most beneficial forms of exercise. Yoga is another option. It requires little space and can be learned quickly with guided instruction. Aerobics and running might suit you better if you prefer a faster pace. All of these forms of exercise will give you a chance to concentrate on your breathing, your body and your rhythm or flow. Swimming is one of my favorites. Of course, with swimming you need a pool or a lake, but swimming laps offers you the opportunity to combine mental, emotional and physical exercise (i.e. meditate while you swim) with your spiritual intent. With swimming, you actually feel the flow all around you. The same is true with T'ai Chi Ch'uan, another form of gentle exercise for health and inner peace.

Be Adventurous:

A wise friend once told me that "it isn't an adventure if you know where you are going." I have remembered these words throughout the years and, as a result, often smile when I might otherwise feel lost. To the pioneering Spirit within us, we are never lost. We are just experiencing an adventure. When we arrive, we know it and learn from it. The truth is, we have no choice in life but to be adventurous because no one actually knows for certain what will happen from one day to the next. Our egos may try to convince us that we can make these predictions, or by playing it safe, we can protect ourselves and sustain our status quo. But sooner or later, we are all met with uncertainty, disruption, sudden changes of plans, bad news, a crisis or an unanticipated string of events. To the enlightened one, this is the only thing that is predictable. Plato once said, "Nothing endures but change." Things will happen. Control is nothing but an illusion. Prophecies and psychic readings, at best, can only forecast potentials. If life were predictable, there would be no point to it. With this in mind, learn to accept the ride you are on. Let it be. Keep your mind open and learn whatever it is you are meant to learn. From here, you can let go of all of the constraints holding you back, open your eyes to new possibilities and actually achieve flow beyond current belief. Use the Ring of Peace to guide you. Awaken to the light of God within you and allow your ascension. This is the second coming of Christ.

Be Playful; Enjoy the Music:

Whenever in doubt, you need look in only one of two places to reconnect with the Holy Spirit. One is art and the other is music. Both are expressions of the heart. Both are soulful in nature. Of course, art and music take on many different forms so you will want to find the expressions best suited to raising consciousness. This can include anything from a beautiful painting to a glorious sunset, an African drum solo to a trickling stream. Combine this with your sense of adventure and you will know when you are connected with Spirit. Your body will respond with the emotion of love. Your eyes may tear up or your body might quiver. You will feel lighter, happier, as if suddenly everything is alright. This is the voice for God reminding us that we are beloved sons and daughters with nothing to fear. We are not alone. Hear it and you will know that you are in the only moment that matters.

Be Forgiving:

When many people think of forgiveness, they think of it in a Newtonian, subject and object way. *I* forgive *you* for hurting me or *you* forgive *me* for acting like a jerk. With this perspective of 'separation,' driven by the ego, we think we are forgiving when we are in fact condemning. We view the forgiveness as being given by one who is above or separate from the other. Even worse, we might agree to forgive but not forget. This approach only hurts the one who cannot let be and let go. When we fail to forgive, we condemn ourselves. This 'mistake' leads to an increase of unconscious guilt and fear in our unconscious mind. In essence, we are teaching ourselves that we are not forgiven and therefore have something to fear. This adds to our karmic debt and delays salvation.

A common theme throughout the teachings of Jesus is forgiveness, an act of unconditional love that demonstrates at a spiritual level that the mistake never happened. Even when Jesus was being crucified, he asked God for forgiveness. Imagine that. He did not condemn Herod or Pilate. He did not condemn Judas. He did not condemn his captors. He could not condemn anyone because he did not see them as separate from himself. He saw only acts of ignorance dictated by the human ego, and to condemn these acts would have been the equivalent of condemning himself. Jesus saw beyond all of this. With the vision of Christ, he saw Christ in everyone, the God-given spiritual essence in all of us. This is the true meaning of forgiveness. We see beyond any acts of human ignorance.

Believe! Be Alive:

It is important during the 'Let Be' step that we surface the underlying beliefs that govern our life. It is from these beliefs that our attitude, our thinking, our feelings, our decisions and our choices follow. Many of these beliefs have been programmed into us from the day we arrived on the planet. Perhaps you recognize certain 'I programming' that includes beliefs about nationality, politics, race, religion, defense, competition, schooling, social circles, work, trust, law, ethics, manners, risk, health, medicine, self-esteem and hundreds of other mental models. These beliefs, or internal programs, result in attitudes, thoughts, feelings, decisions and choices that manifest into our experiences. What are these beliefs? What are the underlying assumptions driving attitude, behavior and results? Pay attention to these beliefs. Are they about the future or are they about the now? Are they about *becoming* or are they about *being*? You will see peace when you are at peace. You will see love when you give love. You will see joy when you are joy. Change your beliefs about the world and you will see a very different world.

Exercise:

Now that we have worked our way backwards through the Ring of Peace, let's go through it frontwards. Begin by identifying 2-3 beliefs that you currently hold in mind, keeping you locked in a vicious circle, a self-fulfilling prophecy of spiritual entrapment. For example, perhaps you have 'programmed' beliefs about certain individuals (family, peers, politicians, etc.) or groups (sects, religions, races, genders, nationalities, etc.) that lead to thoughts of dislike, distrust or injustice. These thoughts then trigger feelings of fear, despair or even rage. From here, you make decisions and choices that impact your life. You decide to attack and fight or withdraw and worry. Either way, you suffer because you are not at peace. You are condemning a brother and in doing so you are condemning yourself. When you condemn a part of the whole, you condemn the whole. You can also substitute a topic or activity for a person or a group (e.g. algebra, paperwork, taxes, exercise, medicine, laundry, yard work, Mondays, snow, broccoli, public speaking, drugs, alcohol, abortion, gay marriage, etc.).

Once you have identified 2-3 beliefs (unquestioned memes, paradigms or mental models you hold to be true) that lead to negative thoughts and feelings, let them go. Give them to God. One way to do this is to close your eyes and visualize a small white light far in the distance. You begin approaching the white light and as you do you see an altar. Place these 'attachments' on the altar, trust in God and visualize them vanishing. Keep in mind, some of these beliefs and attachments can appear to be quite threatening. Remember Abraham's potential sacrifice of his son to God. The lesson is that you do not need to cling to anything temporary because anything temporary is not of God. This includes the human body. Let yourself be free by releasing your perceived need to hold onto people, issues and things.

Another release technique involves using daily affirmations, mantras, chants, meditations and contemplation practices to release negative energy and limiting beliefs from the mind and the body. These healing sounds can be directed at both mind and body concurrently. For example, there are Taoist chants that aim directly at cleansing and harmonizing the five vital organs (kidneys, liver, heart, spleen and lungs), each with corresponding vibrations and energies affecting life balance. I like using these on a daily basis, almost like taking a shower. They are very cleansing in effect. I also meditate daily using ancient Vedic healing sounds that connect to key themes in one's life, like personality, God and relationships. Some of these mantras, healing sounds and chants date back thousands of years, passed along by teachers of teachers. By using these vibrations (the stuff the universe is made of) to connect with the life force, we harmonize and balance our minds, body and Spirit, bringing us closer to God. I highly recommend these practices as a complement to the Ring of Peace.

You will know you have cleared your unconscious and subconscious mind of limiting beliefs when you begin to experience the 'Let See' step. Suddenly, your perspective will change. In fact, it may even vanish. You will no longer feel anxious or spiteful or fearful toward the individuals, groups, topics or activities you selected. You will see the people in a different light. You will find joy in doing the laundry. You will look forward to Mondays and see the benefit of eating broccoli. Your fears and doubts will fade away—about your selected 2-3 items—and you will begin to experience a state of flow and grace. It is like you are now one with the person who annoyed you, one with the laundry, one with the day, one with the vegetable, one with the person you had so much trouble forgiving. There is no longer a perceived separation, because you are seeing beyond the physical, the temporary illusions of the eye.

Practice the Ring of Peace, the four-step model, over and over again. Anytime you find yourself feeling frustrated, upset, stressed or anxious, trace these feelings back upstream to the thoughts you are holding in mind, to your attitude driving these thoughts and to your underlying beliefs causing the attitude. Listen to your heart, the cave of Spirit. Are your thoughts being propelled by the emotion of unconditional love or fear? Be present enough to uncover your thought system and motivation. It is always at this level that trouble begins.

Let Flow (4)

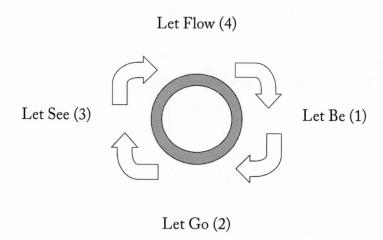

Let See (3)

Let Be (1)

Let Go (2)

CHAPTER SIX

The Forces against Us

'Be the change you want to see in the world.'—Gandhi

When people face change, there is often a tendency to resist. Why is this? What is it about change that people resist? Or is it really 'change' that we resist at all? Could it be something else? After all, people do not resist a pay increase? Nor do people resist changing clothes, changing menus, changing jobs or changing lifestyles. We tend to vote for change at the polls. Nearly every candidate runs a campaign focusing on change. We change our minds and we change our moods, often daily and without effort. In fact, our bodies are designed for change, effortlessly. So if it is not change that we resist, what is it? The answer is deceivingly simple; it is a negative 'perception' of change, driven by the ego. If we see the change as negative or overly disruptive, we tend to resist. If we see it as positive, we tend to accept it. This is a significant force. Our perception of things influences our behavior, one way or another.

The Ring of Peace challenges us to change our perception, ultimately leading us to no perception at all. In other words, as we ascend higher, we leave perception behind and gain true knowledge. With knowledge, there is no need for perception. We rise to a level of 'I am that I am' awareness. Thus, the Ring of Peace is a tool for development and ascension toward pure consciousness. By using the ring, we grow in totality. We see things we have never seen before. We release barriers and limiting beliefs. We experience greater and greater flow in our lives, tapping into the unseen energy and the grace that surrounds us. We empty our minds of useless clutter. But this ascension does not come without resisting forces. The ego will fight back. Anytime fear creeps in, an attitude of attack, retreat or defense follows. The ego will feel threatened because our ascension requires the transcendence of ego. We have to renounce ego to fully embrace Spirit—and the ego knows this! Be prepared for the ego 'force' against you. It exists now, but it coaxes you as an ally as long as it has you convinced that you are one with the ego. This association of ego with self is the very force keeping people in a lower state of consciousness and awareness. It is the root cause of all of fear and doubt. To ascend beyond this fear and doubt, we must renounce and silence the ego and it will not accept this quietly.

When I began this transformation, my ego responded in several different ways. At first, it was curious about the various teachings and applications I was learning and practicing. It was looking at these insights as a way of further expansion of itself. Perhaps my ego could use this information for gain in some way? Maybe I could feel better about myself (ego self) with this profound knowledge. From an ego perspective, I might even be able to impress people, make more money and become famous. Maybe I could use the lessons to improve my body or (ego) self-image. This is the ego's perspective. It constantly seeks to fill a delusional void, a perspective that suggests we are not already whole and complete and one with God.

Once my ego began to experience an unwilling participant, it immediately started throwing more and more turbulence my way. This turbulence manifested in many different ways, but as I became more and more aware of the ego's agenda, I found myself stronger and more capable of letting it go. For example, I would find myself in a long airport line, having to reschedule a cancelled flight from another country. This meant dealing with disruption, inconvenience, hotels, local transportation and not getting home to my family as planned. In the past, this would have triggered a lot of frustration, anger and resentment. I used to wonder, why me? Why now? Why here? Now I use the time to meditate and to people watch. I accept what is, release the ego temptations and negative chatter, and I see the world differently and with flow. Some of my most inspiring thoughts have subsequently come while standing in an airport line, applying the Ring of Peace.

Another example of turbulence I find myself facing frequently is the challenge I get as a teacher from doubtful egos. In one case, a senior level man in the U.S. military scolded me for leading a five day event that he claimed was impossible. He was a member of the team and he insisted that the type of data collection, analysis and interpretation we had planned could not possibly be done in five days. I disagreed peacefully. However, as he pressed on—to the detriment of the team—I could feel my ego trying to rise up, wanting to fight back. How dare he be such a negative influence on the team? What was he trying to accomplish anyway? Was it his intent to undermine the team and humiliate me? If his ego wants to fight, so does mine! Bring it on, says one ego to another. Let's create some drama. The good news is that I was keenly aware of this ego battle and I let my ego know I was savvy to it. Consciously aware, I would not descend to this level. Rather, I calmly asked this executive to leave the team. I could feel his hesitation, fear, doubt and disbelief, so why not offer him an out? He did not have to be on this team, especially if he perceived the mission to be unachievable in the time frame we were committed to. He responded to me by refusing to leave the team—saying he had to be on it—but he quieted down throughout the week. By Friday, when we had successfully achieved the mission, he had little to say at all. Again, more temptation and turbulence presented itself. My ego wanted to say to him, "See, I told you so," but Spirit advised otherwise. Instead, I offered him gratitude. I thanked him in silence for the powerful opportunity he had given me to once again test myself. Without these moments of Truth, we have no opportunity to ascend and awaken. We remain asleep, spinning in drama on a wheel of misfortune, something the Buddhists call Samsara or confused existence.

Turbulence will indeed present itself in many ways. We need to be prepared. Remember, "When the student is ready, the teacher will appear" and "When the *teacher* is ready, the students will appear." We will be tested, just as we are now, but our response will change as we become more 'response-able.' As our ego is tested, and we learn to renounce it as Jesus did, we see these turbulent times differently. This should not be frightening. There is nothing to fear with Spirit—unless we are an ego, which we are not. The ego will be afraid for its life, which means if we experience any fear at all, we know it is our ego feeding the mind with delusions. Spirit is not capable of fear. It knows no fear. So, when we 'are ready,' our students will appear with a variety of challenges. These students, who reflect our own need for learning and understanding, will question us, doubt us, test us and perhaps even provoke us. They may appear as airline attendants, military officers or any number of other shapes and situations. They are here for us and we are here for them. We can respond with an empathetic smile or a vicious stare. We can speak softly with compassion or scream loudly with vengeance. We can act kindly or rudely, positively or negatively, spiritually or selfishly. We have a choice. Just beware of the choice the ego wishes to make. This is a critical first step to elevating our awareness and instilling a deeper sense of inner peace.

To assist you on your journey, consider attending to the following list of characteristics along with those mentioned in the *Let Be* chapter. These overall tendencies are essential to overcoming the forces against us and accelerating the pace of our ascension.

Mind the Will:

Our will is being done. Pay attention to it. Align it with the will of God, with nature, with the Holy Spirit and with the oneness of us all to accelerate your growth. We cannot escape the divine force of life, but we can deny it. We can resist it. We can push it off—temporarily. Just do not be fooled. Our denial becomes part of our karma and we have to 'make adjustments' sooner or later, or continue to 'try again,' if not in this lifetime, in another. Flow requires an alignment of will with the life force. We see this when we let go of denial and resistance. Using the Ring of Peace facilitates this transformation. Let be, let go, let see and let flow.

Minding our will means being spiritually purposeful. It requires that we pay *attention* to our sacred *intention*. Practice contemplating, or meditating, on a daily basis your true intent. What is it you intend? How does this align with Spirit? What motivates your intent? Is it love? Is it peace? Is it harmony? If this is your intent, commit to practicing forgiveness. Forgiveness is salvation. It frees us from the grasp of ego. To practice forgiveness, we must release judgment and condemnation. Again, this is turbulence our ego uses to challenge us. We are put in situations where we are tempted to quickly judge or condemn another soul. If we fall to this temptation, we learn the wrong lesson—and we teach the wrong lesson as well. Be mindful of your will, not your ego's will. Forgive your neighbor. Let go of judgment. Be in touch with your true purpose.

Be Patient:

Patience is a form of peace, the very result we so often seek. When we are patient, we are still. We are at rest. We are resting in peace—a term we might want to use more often with people who are actually alive in Spirit. Patience is a virtue. It puts us in touch with the eternal now, the endless moments of Truth. How often do you hear someone say they do not have time to do certain things that are healthy and productive, like reading enlightening books, listening to inspirational music, looking at illuminating works of art, exercising, meditating, relaxing, or simply enjoying the moment? What better time to do some of these things than when we might otherwise be practicing impatience? Patience is a healthy state of mind. Impatience is not. It has nothing to do with the physical body. It is purely a state of mind, a matter of perspective. Contemplate this the next time you feel impatient. What alternative could you use to replace the attention you are allowing your mind to focus on? There are always alternatives. Perhaps you can find a productive alternative for standing in line, waiting in traffic, sitting in front of a slow computer, awaiting the awakening of a loved one, dealing with mistakes or teaching a challenging student. You may also find that you need to exercise patience with the Ring of Peace. If you are expecting immediate miracles, you may not be aware of the miracles you are already in the middle of. The quick fix mentality of many cultures does not always see the depth and wisdom of the fix. Our world economy is in the middle of one now. So is the planet. In fact, the human race is in the middle of a major 'shift' in consciousness, a true miracle, and many do not exercise the patience or depth to see it. Practice patience with the Ring of Peace and behold the wisdom of the masters.

Be Persevering:

The Ring of Peace, like any other tool, requires practice. It is not enough to intellectualize the model or accept it in a theoretical way. We must experience and feel the changes we are making. There is no other way to know Truth. It cannot be explained. It must be experienced. This can be accomplished through practice and perseverance. It is a lot like learning to ride a bicycle. We may experience a few bumps and bruises as we get started, and we may even take a bad fall well into our practice. These are moments when our ego fights hard and we fall back into an old habit. The Buddhists call these set-backs *Ashrava*. This is the battle of ego. The stronger our ego the more resistance we are likely to experience until we fully renounce the ego. Do not give up. Recognize what is happening and see through it, especially as you ascend higher and your ego shows its true colors. Be mindful that you can and will persevere. This will bring light into your mind which will accompany you as the ego puts forth greater and greater defenses. Trust in this light. It is the light of God. It is what we are made of. We only need to recognize it by clearing away the dark clouds that obstruct it. With perseverance, we gain confidence, credibility and a sense of certainty. We know we are on the right path. We know we can do it. We move beyond doubt.

Trust in God:

We are not alone. We are never alone. There is a life force running through all of us, a force far greater than any individual will. Embrace this force, whatever you choose to call it, and accept its power. We empower ourselves by releasing negative ego denial and embracing the true power within us. No one else can do this for us. We have to do it and we have to decide when. God is infinitely patient and understanding. His will is being done. Our timing is the only thing in question. Recognize the power within you now. We are already empowered. We are meant to flow just like grass is meant to grow green. This is the life force running through and among all of us. Trust in this force and we learn to trust in our true Self—the Oneness that connects us all. Allow the Holy Spirit to fill your heart. Accept the fact that we are loved no matter what we do and that we deserve the very best. We are the prodigal sons of God. Our doubt about this Truth is among the greatest forces we have to overcome to experience enlightenment and inner peace. Let be the power and grace of God. Surrender the ego to God and accept God's one and only will, our true will. Let go of doubt and doubt lets go of us.

Be Generous:

To generate, we must be generous. To be affluent, we must flow. As we find our way along our spiritual path, it is important to recognize that the only way we 'have' anything meaningful is by giving it away. This may or may not mean literally giving it away, but it clearly means giving it up or surrendering it to God. Think of anything meaningful and 'of God' and you can quickly grasp this spiritual Truth. Take love, for example. We gain love by giving love. The same is true of forgiveness, joy, peace and wisdom. Ideas can be shared without loss. So can prayers and positive intentions. This principle poses a direct challenge to the ego belief in scarcity which suggests that the only way to have something is to get it and keep it. This interpretation results in selfishness, greed and the withholding of important information. The ego thinks that if others have what it has it will in some way be diminished. Keep in mind, the ego lives in perpetual fear. The idea of being genuinely and spiritually generous—without some hidden agenda (like showing off)—is threatening to the ego. We experience this as we rise in awareness. The material things that once mattered most no longer seem to matter as much. This does not mean that we do not appreciate them or continue to use them graciously. It just means that we are no longer attached to them in any way. We are 'free' of them.

Being generous means giving our time and attention to others. It means going beyond our ego self to help the world in some way. This could mean volunteering to feed the hungry, coaching young children, assisting the elderly, taking care of a family member, teaching classes or any number of infinite opportunities to serve. These experiences not only bring a sense of joy and support to others but they also bring a profound sense of inner peace to the soul. It is the perfect way to transcend ego and experience a form of enlightenment. Be the miracle you are.

Be Gentle:

In the Taoist practice, students learn to apply no more than four ounces of physical human force in any situation. This includes any related martial art. It is the release of the chi energy—the life force running through us—that enables great power and strength, not physical human force. Learn to use the same gentle approach in everyday life. Learn to *pull* rather than push, especially when parenting, teaching or mentoring. This means gently guiding people to answers with compelling questions and observations. Socrates used this method of discovery brilliantly, leading to what many now call the Socratic teaching method. He guided his pupils, including Plato who went on to teach Aristotle, gently, with questions. When we push opinions, judgments, statements and solutions on people, we often meet with resistance. Never mind that it might be a brilliant answer, the ego in others pushes back and takes a position. One position always leads to another position. The media feeds on this divisive approach, often pitting one opinion against another to make good drama. Conflict sells stories. If a journalist can pit one ego against another on television, the sparks will fly and people will watch. This is now a way of life in many cultures, the exact opposite of inner peace. The media actually looks for and publishes turmoil, giving people a chance to choose sides, often without any facts at all.

Being gentle means ultimately transcending the win/lose, us/them, right/wrong, yes/no judgments that dominate the front pages. It means letting go of opinion and judgment, the language of the ego. This does not mean giving up thought or relinquishing decisions. It just means moving beyond *attachment* to positions. Again, this brings a sense of inner peace to the soul as we are no longer anguished over an unfilled desire or loss. As Jesus said, 'The meek shall inherit the earth.' The meek are at peace. The meek are gentle. The meek are strong. The meek are wise. The meek are not careless or apathetic. On the contrary, the meek are loving and compassionate. The meek just do not *mind* the outcome. The meek live joyfully and lovingly in any situation, seeing beyond doubt. For the body to be at peace, the mind must be at peace. If we do not mind, we are at peace.

Be Honest:

Dishonesty is another significant force against us that only we can release. If we choose denial over truth, manipulation over fact or blame over ownership, we enter into a victim consciousness. The ego loves this because it adds to the drama. Why not deny the facts? Why not manipulate the data? Why not find an excuse? Everyone does it. The problem here is that there is no hiding from universal Truth. It abides deep in our subconscious mind, often surfacing just enough to trigger sleepless nights, imbalanced behavior or challenging illnesses. As Jesus said, the Truth shall set you free. Hold this reality in mind as you learn to accept what is, release what is not and witness the peace of God. It is from this awareness of eternal bliss that we harmonize with the universe and experience flow. To be in flow we must see the flow. Our spiritual enlightenment relies on spiritual Truth and our ability to see this Truth depends on our willingness to be honest, first with ourselves and then with the world we live in.

I like to think of the Ring of Peace as a symbol of love and spiritual commitment. By accepting it, we are expressing our intent to ascend beyond our limited perception of self to the glory of God within us. The seeds are already planted. By attending to them, we are nurturing our spiritual growth. By committing to them, we are demonstrating the courage required to shift human consciousness—a shift from ego domination to spiritual illumination.

The seven characteristics highlighted in this chapter are necessary to bring the ring to life. It is not the tool that enlightens us. It is our use of the tool. Like any tool, we can use it or abuse it. We can also let it sit idle, collecting dust like many useful tools do. Challenge yourself on this. Do not let the Ring of Peace sit idle. Demonstrate your will, be patient and persevere. Trust in God to help you through any turbulence and beware of the battle of the ego. Be generous and gentle and honest with yourself. These characteristics bring integrity to our use of the tool and facilitate our ascension.

CHAPTER SEVEN

Miracle 'Kaizens'

'I am that I am.'—Jesus

When we are in communion with our true essence, our divine spiritual Self, we are living life at full potential. We are in flow. We are that we are. We are without fear. We are without doubt. We are without any perceived need for approval, control or security. We know that there is no sickness or death and that anything temporary is without true value. This is a state of grace. It is our natural essence, our flow. It is home. It is heaven. It is joy. It is peace. Ego and evil have left our consciousness. When we are in this state, we carry no jealousy or anger. We carry no judgment. We feel relaxed. We laugh and we smile—a lot!

Challenges will always come and go. The state of grace does not mean that we have no yin moments. This would defy the laws of the universe. It simply means that we approach and experience these challenges with a different mindset, a state of compassion and grace. We see through and beyond the yin moments to the reason why they must exist. Consider these moments to be opportunities for expressing unconditional love and forgiveness. When someone annoys you, see them as doing their job. They are simply giving you a chance to test yourself, to change your mind—perhaps even to smile. Consider that on a soul level, the exchange is taking place in order for both of you to grow. Consider that the incident is not some spontaneous, unfortunate event, but an 'agreement' that you both made at a soul level long ago. This is karma. It is action and reaction. It is an imprint or memory at the soul level that we carry with us until we learn to balance the scale and spiritually let it go. We are not victims at all. We participated in creating our own debt, perhaps long ago. Make amends now. Let go of the ego self and bring harmony and balance back into your life. Witness the wisdom and perfection in every human exchange for the spiritual meaning it carries.

The same holds true with work challenges. The nature of the workplace today is to do more with less. People often become intimidated by these increasing demands, perhaps even angry, but it does not help. Chances are anger only makes it worse. When we become angry or bitter, we hurt ourselves. We convince ourselves that anger is real, sometimes even rationalizing its value. Listen to Spirit. Be still. Open your mind. Allow yourself to see the wisdom and compassion and higher intelligence of God. It is all around us. Let go of the ego constraints, and see with new eyes. We have nothing to fear. We have nothing to be angry about. We get through these challenges. We evolve and grow. Remember, there is no problem without a solution. We see it when we believe it.

In 2007, I was asked to help facilitate a 'kaizen event' with a company in Portugal. A kaizen event is a fast, targeted process improvement, usually conducted by a team over a three to five day period. The Japanese word *kaizen* essentially means 'good change' and the idea of an event is to make good change quickly. This particular event was challenging and memorable. To keep this facility open and preserve hundreds of jobs, the team had to find a way to run a seven day continuous operation in five days per week without any capital expenditure. We had five days to figure it out. This was a mission beyond doubt.

When I arrived, the team was assembled but clearly concerned. Some were in a state of complete disbelief. How were we going to come up with that much 'free capacity?' The operation was already running a 24/7 schedule and there was no idle equipment—or so the team thought. We set to work following a disciplined process improvement methodology. We gathered facts, prepared process maps, crunched numbers, analyzed data, developed alternatives, tested hypotheses and drew conclusions—all reinforcing what some team members seemed to expect all along. The mission appeared to be impossible. The plant was destined to close. It was Monday afternoon and people were feeling anguished, so we decided to take a walk. We started on the factory floor, investigating every piece of equipment involved. The primary constraint operation was obvious, a specific type of chemical reactor. There was no doubt about it. To achieve a five day schedule, the team needed to come up with an additional reactor—fast! Of course, another constraint was having no money to purchase additional equipment and these reactors were very, very expensive. We pressed on searching for hidden capacity within existing reactors, but no such capacity could be found. The team turned to me for help and guidance. There had to be light somewhere in this tunnel. I asked to see their warehouse. This seemingly odd request was met with a blend of blank stares and raised eyebrows. What could we possibly find in the warehouse that might solve this problem? The warehouse is mostly full of spare parts and junk. Ten minutes later, expressions changed from hopeless disbelief to astonished disbelief. There in front of us was the exact chemical reactor we needed, still in a crate and never before used. We were back in the game. No one was quite sure where the reactor came from or how it got there, but it was there. Once again, I witnessed what many would call a miracle. We had what we needed to move forward—a change of mind and a key piece of equipment. By Friday, we had a plan in place to keep the facility open and the necessary changes were already underway. This meant clearing several other hurdles and secondary constraints, but these tasks seemed effortless once we had some momentum. The team rejoiced. The mission did indeed take all of us beyond doubt.

I enjoy facilitating kaizen events for this very reason. It is a wonderful way to teach people to experience different results by altering perception. I remember one event in Michigan where our mission was to take a nineteen hour process down to four hours within five days. To make the mission even more challenging, this particular process had a range of fifteen hours to twenty-nine hours, meaning that no one ever knew how long the process was actually going to take. This variation in time made it especially difficult for the people in the planning and scheduling departments, not to mention the people directly involved in the process.

We kicked off the session on Monday morning by reviewing the project charter with the team, including the four hour goal by Thursday. By mid-morning break on the first day, one of the senior team members approached me with serious concerns. He explained that several other team members had expressed extreme doubt about our mission. Through their eyes, the idea of a four-hour goal was ludicrous, especially since the last sample we reviewed took twenty-seven hours. How were we supposed to take a process that long and complex and complete it within four hours by Thursday? Perfect, I thought to myself. We have an opportunity to change minds, not just the process in focus. I shared my optimism with the senior team member, who shrugged his shoulders and wandered off shaking his head.

When the team reconvened, there was little doubt about the doubt. It reminded me of a group of people feeling lost in the dark without any sense of direction. Someone needed to turn on a light and point the way to the door. Otherwise, it was utter confusion and chaos. By Tuesday afternoon, after breaking through many limiting beliefs, memes and mental barriers, we found a light switch. Then we found a door, giving us some sense of direction. This was followed by hope. Next, we began charting a course to turn hope into promise and promise into conviction. By Wednesday afternoon, we had a detailed plan of action and we were preparing for a 'test flight' on Thursday. More importantly, we had a team of people who had gone from complete skepticism and doubt on Monday to high expectations and enthusiasm by Wednesday. The pilot on Thursday took four hours and twenty minutes. Given the dramatic improvement, one might now have thought that the new process design was a spectacular success. In fact, the executive vice president for this billion dollar company visited the pilot demonstration and expressed his elation with the team and their spirited progress. The improvement was worth millions of dollars in freed up capacity and a vast improvement in working conditions. This helped, but the team was now disappointed in missing their target. I found myself laughing. Here was a team that on Monday couldn't imagine doing the process in less than fifteen hours, and now they are kicking themselves for accomplishing it in just over four hours.

When people seek to understand human motivation and behavior, they often find themselves looking to the teachings of Abraham Maslow and the 'hierarchy of needs.' This is a model showing how people are motivated by 'higher' needs once more basic needs are met. In other words, once we have our physical needs taken care of (priority #1), our sense of security needs covered (priority #2) and our social needs satisfied (priority #3), we find ourselves thinking we need more. We want to feel valued and important (priority #4). We want to feel good about who we are and what we are doing. We want to feel like we matter. For many people, it is this perceived need for self-esteem and approval that motivates behavior. It is what drives many people to put forth extra effort in school, at work or on an athletic field.

These efforts stem from a perceived need to fill a void, receive recognition or 'be somebody.' This is in fact an ego need driven by a sense of doubt because at the spiritual level we are already whole and complete. We are one with God. Perfection needs nothing. It is simply the ego in all of us that thinks otherwise.

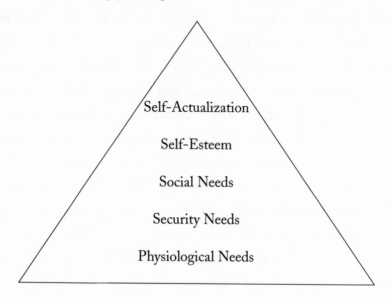

Maslow's Hierarchy of Needs

Given this common human ego need, countless organizations around the world have sought to differentiate themselves from the norm by tapping into self-esteem. These companies go beyond paying people (a physiological need) and offering insurance benefits, safety programs, training and social activities (security and social needs). The best organizations seek ways to help employees feel valued and important—like winners! This is a unique competitive advantage. It is a powerful way to motivate people and cultivate improvement, like running kaizen events, for example. This approach fosters the generation of ideas, the flow of talent, the growth of the people and a spirit of innovation. In these work cultures, people are upbeat and excited, not because they have the highest pay or the best benefit plan, but because the environment brings out the best in them. There is an alignment of purpose, a positive connection of energy.

This brings us to the top of Maslow's Hierarchy of Needs, self-actualization, a level few organizations have even begun to understand because very few leaders understand it themselves. To understand self-actualization we must understand true human essence and potential because self-actualization means *realizing* our full potential as human beings. It means actualizing who and what we really are—our true Self living in human form. This means transcending the ego self and liberating our spiritual Self. The challenge is this: On a human ego level, how are we to know our true potential? How are we to measure it? What are we really capable of? Is it our ego's definition of self, or is it our true spiritual Self? If it is the ego's definition, we can never get there because the ego believes in scarcity and lack. We can never reach our full potential because we will always be missing something. The ego sees realizing full potential as a moving target, anything but stillness and peace. We can never be at rest or at peace because our ego mind is telling us we are incomplete. As a result, we tend to become attached to our physiological, safety and social needs, resistant to letting go, and we continue our search for recognition, approval and control. We are trapped by the illusions of the ego mind.

Some organizations have done a remarkable job cultivating a spirit of growth, innovation and transformation. One in particular comes to mind, a meat packing company. At the time I got involved, the company was experiencing an employee turnover rate of over 400%. This means that on average the entire workforce changed four times per year, resulting in a significant loss of capability and skill. Not every employee would leave. In fact, some very capable and hard-working people stayed behind, a real blessing for this company, but a tremendous burden for these loyal people who had to continually retrain new employees.

Some people would argue that it is just not desirable to work in a meat packing company. It is standard in the industry to turn people over frequently because of the challenging work environment. This was the rationale among some managers at the company, most especially the managers with the highest turnover in their departments. When I was first invited to help, the request was for some team-building training. I get this request a lot. In this case, I asked the two senior executives who contacted me if they had attempted any team-building training before. They answered yes, approximately one year earlier. When asked what happened, they explained that it was the training company that fell short. I then asked if they had made any changes to the employee work *systems* to cultivate and reward more cooperation and teamwork. The answer was no. In other words, this company had attempted to solve a symptom without addressing any root causes. This is like taking one shower and expecting to sustain personal hygiene indefinitely. It does not work. How many people do you know who have gone off to a team-building retreat, only to return to a system of isolated and independent work? The training washes away quickly if there is no reinforcement. Good people in a bad system are demoralized by the bad system.

I suggested to these executives that they reconsider their strategy, which they resisted, so I then politely removed myself as a candidate for the training. I had no interest in being the next scapegoat. Several days later, the president of this company asked me to meet with him personally to discuss alternative strategies. He was quite aware of the 'waste' being generated by the heavy turnover and was eager to explore other options. He also admitted that he was quite surprised that a consultant would 'walk away' from (or *let go* of) prospective work. These discussions led to a change in strategy and a 'walk the talk' team approach to problem-solving and process improvement. In less than one year, a focused, aligned and empowered team—through a series of kaizens—designed and implemented a *voluntary (pull)* skill-based compensation system to motivate, recognize and reward on-going learning and application. This meant that employees could empower themselves, within the parameters of the system, to advance their knowledge, ability and pay. In addition, each employee had to share their knowledge and skill with others (teach) in order to advance to the next level. As a result, employee turnover fell to below 60% annually, a benchmark in the industry at the time. More importantly, the people who did join the company and later moved on to another company did so with a whole new sense of responsibility and accomplishment. Those who stayed behind experienced the power of teamwork as well. Where there is light, there can be no darkness. The key is finding the switch.

The last kaizen event I will share now is a 'David and Goliath' story. David, in this case was my client, and Goliath was a major customer of theirs. In terms of size, David was clearly a spec among approximately 10,000 other suppliers to Goliath. Our mission was to conduct a kaizen event with Goliath, leading to mutual changes to a process both companies depended on. This meant travelling to England, where Goliath would host the event. My client was quite nervous about this exchange, but prepared diligently. In fact, both parties were a bit nervous because neither had ever experienced a 'joint kaizen event.' On top of this, many of the participants had never met before so it was especially intimidating for some of the team members early in the week. We set to work, mapping the process in focus and exploring the data that accompanied it. Rather than push for change—especially with Goliath, we used the data and analysis tools to 'pull' people in and cultivate discovery. By the end of the week, we had identified and approved multiple significant changes, leading to measureable improvements in both companies. In fact, Goliath discovered a need to make more changes than those implemented by David. This came as quite a surprise to my client, due to the doubt that initially travelled with them. Once again, we journeyed beyond doubt and found the adventure quite enlightening. To top it off, Goliath awarded David with one of their top ten supplier awards among the 10,000 suppliers and increased their orders for business. Goliath also discovered that the improvements made to this 'joint' process could be rolled out to thousands of other suppliers, reducing waste, redundancies and unnecessary costs. In this story, David did not slay Goliath. He enlightened him.

CHAPTER EIGHT

Ask a Mystic

*'Thousands of candles can be lit from a single candle,
and the life of the candle cannot be shortened. Happiness
never decreases by being shared.'—Buddha*

Over the years, countless questions have come my way about some of the topics covered in this book. The purpose of this chapter is to share some of these questions, along with a written response. If you have a specific question of your own, please feel free to submit it to *askamystic@comcast.net*.

Question: What do you consider to be the single greatest barrier or constraint to inner peace?

When Jesus was being crucified, he asked for forgiveness—not for himself, but for the people challenging him. He said, 'Forgive them for they know not what they do.' He did not condemn them. Jesus was not capable of condemnation because it was not a part of his consciousness. He recognized their ignorance and sought forgiveness so that they might be free of suffering. The Buddha said essentially the same thing: that ignorance is the root cause to all suffering. When we hold grievances against one another, *we* suffer. These grievances prevent us from experiencing inner peace. They make us angry and spiteful, leading to drama and discontent. Our ignorance breeds judgment which leads to anger and conflict, attack and defense. We then find ourselves spinning in a vicious circle, the exact opposite of the Ring of Peace. We do not let be. We fight and resist. We do not let go. We cling to positions. We do not see beyond the conflict. We become clouded in judgment. And we do not flow with the divine forces of nature. We become constrained and stressed. Therefore, to experience true inner peace, we have to practice the Ring of Peace repeatedly. We grow out of ignorance by accepting what is and learning from it. We learn to see things differently by letting go of the forces against us—principally the ego, its attachments and its judgment. And we experience flow and grace and compassion when it is all that exists in our consciousness, our mind's eye. What do I see as the single greatest barrier or constraint to inner peace? It is our ignorant denial and resistance to letting be, letting go, letting see and letting flow.

Question: What do you consider to be the most important step in the 4-step model?

I have described the model as having four steps for the sole purpose of explanation. Indeed, it has only one step, your decision to use it. The model is holistic, dynamic and universal. As such, there is no single most important step in the Ring of Peace. Any one step without the others is incomplete and ineffective. Beware of the ego tendency to compare and contrast things, using labels to divide and isolate. Thinking in such a way is another form of separateness. Use the model in its entirety every time. Consider each 'cycle' a step if you must. For example, think of a conflict you are suffering from right now and practice the model all the way through. Let be the conflict. Do not deny or resist it. Just let it be. Feel it. Accept it. Seek to understand it. Look deeply into yourself beyond the ego, beyond doubt. Remember that the ego will deny and dismiss any responsibility for the conflict or suffering you experience, instead putting the blame on someone or something else. Listen to Spirit, your connection to God. This will tell you what *you* need to let go of to see your situation differently. Stop worrying about what others have to do, or not do. Allow yourself to take personal responsibility for enlightenment. You will know you have found the 'root cause' when you let it go and see the situation entirely different. You may even find yourself laughing when you otherwise might have been screaming or crying. This is a moment of flow, an experience of grace and enlightenment. You have just now seen and felt the light. This is the miracle of the model. It helps us transcend our ego self and our limited perspective of life and begin to see and experience the world in a new and inspiring way.

Question: I seem to be surrounded by a lot of negative energy at work. People are frequently complaining, comparing and arguing with one another. How can I overcome this? It is so easy to fall into the same trap and respond in kind.

We cannot be surrounded by what your ego interprets as negative energy without simultaneously being surrounded by the potential for the opposite, positive energy. This is the yin and yang of life. It is the natural way, the perfect harmony and balance of the universe. For every force, there is an equal and opposite force. For every position, there is an opposing position, often called denial. Be the alternative many unconscious minds deny. Be the light. Do not deny the positive force that offsets the negative force. Notice that when a light goes on in a dark room, the light overcomes the darkness. We have a choice in every situation. We are able to respond differently, but we must be conscious of this choice and make it deliberately. What you are seeing and judging is a misperception of the ego. Consider each 'dark' moment an opportunity to shine your light, to be positive. Without these moments we would have no real opportunity to test ourselves, to help one another, to elevate our consciousness. Feel these moments without judgment. Let them be. Do not fight them or resist them. Accept them and witness the ignorance and suffering beneath them. Experience the 'dis-ease' that accompanies dark, negative thought and then let it go. See the alternative and be the alternative. Bring comfort and grace to the moment. In time, people will notice that you are behaving differently. In fact, they may begin to wonder how it is that you do not get agitated and upset. Why does nothing seem to bother you? How do you handle stress so gracefully? Where do you get such confidence, equanimity and inner peace? This is your opportunity to lead. We inspire others by being in-Spirit ourselves. However, do not expect others to immediately see and accept this light. It may not yet be a part of their consciousness. If they have not yet learned to let be and let go, they may not yet be able to see and experience the light that follows. This can test your patience and quite possibly lead you to consider an alternative work environment. Do not give up. Do not mind the resistance. See the wisdom in the situation. Learn what you are meant to learn. We are always exactly where we are supposed to be in the moment. The ego will fight you on this, but recognize that you are a part of something far greater than the ego. You are in the situation to learn whatever it is you need to learn at the spiritual level and pass the lessons on. This is your karma. Be aware of it and then transcend it. Be a teacher of teachers. Hold the light for others, in whatever field or line of work you serve. This is your true purpose in life.

Question: My boss is a far cry from enlightened. What can I do to avoid frequent frustration and disappointment?

You are not frustrated or disappointed because of your boss. Your ego only wants you to think this is the case. The real case is that you are *allowing* your boss to frustrate and disappoint you, ego to ego. Your ego is directing you to fix blame on someone or something other than yourself. This is how the ego operates. It seeks conflict. It relishes in drama. Your boss's ego may in fact be playing the same game. Perhaps your boss assumes that he must exercise his positional authority over you to feel better about himself. This type of behavior stems from ignorance, not knowing any better. Ignorance is the root cause of all suffering. From it grows fear, doubt, disbelief and resistance. This spawns shame, guilt, apathy, grief, regret, selfishness, anger, jealousy and pride. It also leads to stress, frustration and disappointment. Look within yourself. Why do you feel the way you do? What do you see in your boss and why do you see it? What assumptions, thoughts and emotions are you holding onto that lead to your current feelings? What exactly are you thinking about your boss? Does the emotion of fear interact with these thoughts? How would you feel if you let go of these thoughts and replace the emotion of fear with the emotion of love? These questions will lead you into the release phase of the Ring of Peace, where you can let go and elevate your awareness. Perhaps then you will begin to see the conflict, pain and suffering your boss is experiencing. This enlightened vision then leads to compassion, forgiveness and grace, a state of flow. From here, you may or may not choose to stay in this relationship, but there will be no hard feelings. You will be at peace. You will be free of the mental, emotional and spiritual anguish you carry with you now. You can leave anytime you want. The key is to leave in peace, without condemnation.

Question: My daughter is dating someone I do not approve of. He is lazy, disrespectful and sloppy. My wife and I have both expressed our disapproval, but our daughter resists our opinion and advice. It seems as if we are reinforcing something we do not want. What can you suggest?

Your ego is making the matter personal, between you, your daughter and her boyfriend. As a result you suffer. Your ego is disapproving of a brother and you are using a 'push' approach in imposing this judgment on your daughter. Your ego seeks control and is expressing doubt over the situation. Your daughter is pushing back, ego to ego, perception versus perception, judgment against judgment. Use the Ring of Peace to break this vicious circle and move beyond doubt. Let be the current situation. Recognize that it is what it is for a reason. Seek to understand this reason. It may be a lesson for you, your daughter and her boyfriend. Accept the current state. Your daughter is your daughter. Do not try to 'change' her. She is who she is. Love her without condition. Do not try to change or control her boyfriend. He is who he is. Let it be. Look for the light in him, even if you do not approve of his (ego) behavior. On a spiritual level, he is just as much a son of God as you are. Most of all, let go of making this situation personal, you against some other human being. Focus instead on the *relationship* between you, your daughter and her boyfriend. Ask your daughter (pull, do not push) if the relationship brings out the best in her. Does she feel motivated and alive when they are together? Is the relationship trustworthy, balanced and healthy? How is she inspired by the relationship? You may also want to express your observations, feelings and concerns about the *relationship*—without condemnation—and the behaviors that concern you. Remind your daughter that you love her unconditionally and you want the very best for her. Let her know that you have concerns for her safety and well-being, and then let these doubts go. Do not attach yourself to her choice. Let be and let go. She will hear your words and witness your grace when you release any distrusting or doubtful (ego) thoughts from your consciousness. This will take courage on your part, a key characteristic of inspirational leadership. Take the lead. Be the light. Soon you will see the situation differently. You will see why your daughter is making this choice. Your ego may not like the boyfriend, but you will now be beyond that. You will see the value in the learning and the freedom that comes with it. Your daughter may or may not choose to stay with this soul, but your relationship with yourself and with her will be sound. Your relationship with her boyfriend may change as well. Once he realizes that he is no longer being evaluated and judged on his every move, he may warm up to you and show more respect. If not, your daughter will take note. If she feels your love, rather than your attempt at control and criticism, she will not want to see you hurt.

Question: I think fear and doubt are important human feelings, often times motivating people to achieve higher levels of performance. What is the risk in eliminating these feelings? Do people risk becoming complacent?

Fear and doubt are the perception and the language of the ego. On a limited scale, the ego thought system can help one rise to a level of pride, especially in school or in the workplace, but pride itself is a barrier to enlightenment and inner peace. Pride is a higher level of consciousness than shame or guilt or apathy, but it is by no means the end of our spiritual journey. In fact, pride marks the end of our *ego journey* but it precedes our true spiritual journey. In other words, it is the very feeling we need to let go of to ascend to the higher levels of communion, limitless joy, inner peace and spiritual enlightenment. This means that fear and doubt may temporarily appear to motivate higher levels of performance, but they increase the risk of becoming complacent at the same time. Here is how this works: Accompanying the feeling of pride is denial, resistance, separation and a new level of complacency. With pride, people deny a different perspective might be true. With pride, people resist alternative points of view. With pride, people compete and see the world as separate, us versus them, one is better than another. Schools and nations draw lines in the sand and fly flags in the spirit of pride and competition. This limited perspective of pride, when taken to extremes, is the very cause of disharmony, conflict and even war. Remember, the underlying emotion driving pride is fear. When people are proud, they are still subconsciously afraid. With unconditional love, there is no need for pride. To ascend spiritually, people need to let go of pride and the fear and doubt that comes with it. It is a barrier to advancement and enlightenment. It is a blindfold to be removed. It is a form of complacency many people are not even aware of. It is the equivalent of trying to move forward in life by looking back. Let it go and see with new eyes. Do not let the ego, with its fear and doubt, hold you back. Experience pride and then let it go.

Question: I still have a hard time with the concept of letting go of my ego. It seems to me that my ego has served me well, especially in business. Why should I let that go?

Much of the world we live in today is dominated by the doubtful ego. In this realm, it appears that fear motivates some people to set goals, win at any cost and seek material gain. We see it in business. We see it in sports. We see it in politics. We even see it in religious disputes. Yet, when people are filled with doubt and driven by fear, they *close* their minds to new insights and revelation. They avoid acceptance. They deny Spirit. They resist adventure and uncertainty. They 'stay within the lines of (their) society,' seeking approval, control and safety because they do not feel at peace within themselves. This perceived sense of emptiness may drive some people to achieve more in work life, as evaluated by the ego, but because any perception of emptiness is an illusion, it cannot be filled. With each promotion or pay increase, the ego demands more. This adds to the subconscious feeling of emptiness and guilt, promoting more fear and doubt, in this case the fear of losing what one has attained. Fear and doubt also infiltrate the family life. While it may drive certain temporary behaviors in the workplace, fear and doubt can destroy the trust and cohesion needed in a healthy family. Spiritual fulfillment goes beyond all of this, beyond doubt. When we let go of ego, including all of its negative energies including worry and stress, we find ourselves in a new place, a place where we are whole and complete. We think more clearly. We are more aware of what really matters and what doesn't, what helps and what hurts spiritually. We feel alive and free, and we act with much more confidence and grace.

Question: I have always been taught to set goals for the future using a 'SMART' framework (Specific, Measurable, Attainable, Relevant and Timed). You say we should set goals for the present, using a 'Be' rather than 'Become' approach. Can you explain this in more detail and provide an example? I am still not sure I agree with it.

You can still use a SMART framework for setting goals with a 'Be' approach. The difference is in how you are *communicating* these goals to yourself and to the universe, both consciously and subconsciously. This makes all the difference in the world. If you project your desired state out into the future using a 'Become' approach, as if it is *not* happening now, you send a message of lack and deprivation. This is why so many people give up after awhile. Their goals continue to elude them and they grow weary, or they temporarily achieve them only to find they are unfulfilling or unsustainable. Thinking in the now, in terms of *being* rather than *becoming*, means that you are reinforcing your current ability to achieve your goals on an immediate and on-going basis. Take losing weight, for example. Rather than setting a SMART goal like 'I will lose ten pounds within three months,' try telling yourself (using a daily mantra or affirmation) 'I am now easily attaining my optimal body weight (10 pounds less?)' or 'I now have the knowledge, determination and discipline to exercise, eat right and lose ten pounds effortlessly' or 'I give myself permission right now to lose any unnecessary weight and live my life with more energy, passion and balance.' This type of goal setting generally begins with words like 'I am, I have or I allow myself' to be effective and successful immediately. It transcends ego goals and taps into the universal, spiritual energy that keeps us all alive and healthy to begin with. These goals can be specific, measurable, attainable, relevant and timed. The difference is in the timing. When we know we are making the right choices in the eternal present, any gap that exists (between current state and clearly defined future state visualized in the now) is corrected by an energy field that goes far beyond the ego. This means we are trusting in the will of God and the power of the Holy Spirit, the life force that sustains us, to heal us. Heal your mind and your body and behavior will follow. The ego will resist this spiritual Truth, but the ego is playing mind games. See past this and be thankful for who and what you are right now. The same approach can be used in the workplace. While your boss or organization may require you to set written quarterly or annual goals—to provide a sense of direction and accountability—execution is always performed in the present. We execute our actions in the now. So even if setting written, strategic goals and plans is part of the job, we can translate these goals into immediate feelings, actions and behaviors to channel the energy into success. As Gandhi put it, "Be the change you want to see in the world." Allow the chi energy to help you with your body weight or your business plan. Trust the life force. Feel your optimal Self in the now. Relinquish doubt and be in flow. Take responsibility for what you see and do and allow the universe to close any gaps. This is not abrogating responsibility. It is being wise about responsibility.

Question: I really struggle with letting things be. How can this be a positive step?

Genuine acceptance of God's will brings joy. Resistance to what is natural does not. Joy is positive. It is the Truth. It is what is meant to be. Embrace this. Accept the joy that flows within you. The present moment cannot be changed. Resisting it is what brings disharmony and discontent, first to your mind and then to your body. Your denial and dislike of what is happening now will not change it. It will only aggravate your ego. You are attached to a vision in your mind's eye that you think does not exist in the present moment and this frustrates you. It stirs up feelings of lack and deprivation. Your mental attachment to an illusion leads to your discontent and costs you inner peace in the moment. A better alternative is to accept what is, feel it, learn from it and use it to let go of the causes that create unrest. For example, if you are upset with someone's behavior and this stirs up feelings of jealousy and anger, stop and contemplate what thoughts and emotions you hold in mind that make you feel this way. Chances are, you are seeing behavior that contradicts what you would like to see—which is an ego judgment on your part. Why is your ego making this judgment? What is this telling you about yourself? Are you seeing behavior in someone else that reflects your own inner doubts and insecurities? Are you trying to control the situation without control? What might happen to your own state of mind if you released these doubts? Alter your perception and you alter your world.

Question: How do you let go of opinion and judgment and still function effectively in today's world? I just don't get it.

Whenever we hold a position in mind we immediately create its opposite, often in the subconscious mind. It doesn't matter what the position is. There is always an opposite position. This means that we are creating doubt in our own subconscious mind by telling ourselves that one position is right and the other is wrong. On the conscious level, we are convinced we are right. But at the subconscious level, the opposite presents itself as a viable option. Without facts and the true knowledge of God, it might be equally as true. This divides the mind and creates tension and conflict within us, often at a level we are not aware of. As Jesus taught, 'No man can serve two masters.' The ego insists on opinion and judgment. Spirit relies on knowledge, a level beyond perception and perspective. This does not mean that we are no longer equipped to make decisions. On the contrary, we are better equipped to make honest, genuine, unbiased decisions for the better good. The issue you face may be more self-preserving, meaning "I am expected to take sides or I risk some form of perceived punishment." Perhaps you think your boss will fire you or you will lose face or sacrifice something you see as valuable. This enrolls us in the battle of egos. We live in a very ego-centric world, clearly capable of killing one another by the hundreds of thousands, stealing from one another from Wall Street to Main Street and destroying the planet. This is not sane behavior, yet it all stems from biased opinion and judgment. Free yourself from taking positions and sides, by 'not minding.' This does not mean you do not care. You care deeply, but you care without attachment. This is what compassion is all about. You can live peacefully in any circumstance while you continue to work for the common good.

Question: How are we to be at peace when the world is not at peace? People are starving. The planet is suffering. I do not feel comfortable letting this be.

How can the world be at peace if you are not at peace? By carrying these thoughts in your conscious mind, you are adding to the suffering. There is no need for this. Free yourself of judgment, criticism and doubt and then channel your thoughts into positive action. Send money to a homeless shelter. Buy a meal for people in need. Plant a tree. Rethink, recycle and reuse. These are actions with sacred intent, acts of love. They go a long way in easing perceived pain by moving the world forward in a positive direction. Complaining and affixing blame does just the opposite. It adds to suffering through the collective unconsciousness of humankind.

Question: I have a tendency to get angry a lot and sometimes I don't even know why. I know I need to uncover the thinking underlying this tendency and let the thoughts go, but what do I do if I don't know the origin of the problem?

The origin of anger is judgment. Judgment comes from ignorance, and ignorance is of the ego. Let go of the ego and renounce its insane perspective and you will be free of anger. This does not mean that you will not stumble and fall back into an ego habit from time to time, but by being conscious of your thoughts you can eventually eliminate these anger tendencies indefinitely. Guard your thoughts carefully. Remain conscious. The ego will challenge you, especially as it feels more threatened. Just remember, the ego is never right. It does not love you. It is not capable of love. Anger is never justified, despite the ego's objection to this spiritual Truth. When you judge, it is your ego forming an opinion, usually about another ego or a temporary situation. Given the ego is always wrong, how can your ego interpretation of behavior be any more right than the ego behavior you are observing? Remember that Spirit, your absolute connection with God, does not recognize ego. To Spirit it is as if the ego does not even exist (to the ego's dismay). Thus, the only thing Spirit sees is the absolute connection with God that we all share, our divine being, our oneness. It cannot be fooled by the ego. The Holy Spirit cannot doubt us or condemn us because He sees only the perfection we all carry deep within us. When we learn to see one another in this way, it is reflected back to us. In other words, by seeing the innocence, beauty and grace in others, we see it in ourselves, freeing us from any unconscious anger, guilt, grief and doubt we have buried away. We manifest the vision of Christ by seeing it in others.

Question: Someone very close to me denies he has an ego. He insists that he is happy, healthy and wise. I want to believe this but his chronic boredom, anger, judgment and criticism tell a different story. What can I do to help?

Recognize first that it is your own ego making this judgment. You are denying Truth just as much as he is, subconsciously reinforcing the illusion. Every human being is born with an ego. It is our animal instinct. It is what triggers such feelings as 'fight or flight,' fear, possessiveness, jealousy, judgment, control and anger. It is the ego that feels incomplete, seeks approval from others and holds grudges. It is the ego that becomes bored and seeks external stimulus. Spirit has no need for any of this. Your friend may not yet recognize this, but perhaps neither do you.

If you did, you would know that there is really only one way to handle this situation. Love your friend unconditionally. Give him your silent blessing. Heal him by healing yourself and the relationship you have with him. See the light of God in him. Let be the situation and let go of your judgment and attachment. You will see with new eyes and flow with the emotion of love. In this state, you will gain empathy and understanding and use this increased awareness to manage yourself more effectively. In time, your friend may take notice and perhaps even ask you about the change in your behavior. There will be a greater attraction between you. But you are not attached to this reaction. You are not attached to any outcome. The healing has taken place when it exists in your mind. You have freed yourself, forgiven yourself by forgiving another and fostered communion with your friend. Peace is within you as well as between you, even if it is not yet acknowledged by your friend.

Question: I recently lost my job, most of my savings and now I face potential bankruptcy. How can I find inner peace at a time like this?

You can find inner peace any time you want. It is not hiding. Inner peace is a state of mind, a natural state of mind. It is what we are without the ego. It is where we came from and it is where we are meant to be. It is our spiritual essence. When times are tough, we are being tested. Each test leaves us with lessons learned and karmic imprints. We cannot alter the test once it has been given, although there are things we can do to avoid certain tests and accelerate our learning. Once the test is given, it is as it is. The question now is how do we choose to respond? One option is to go with the ego, to worry, to become stressed, to hold onto doubt and grief, and to see the experience as negative. Maybe there is someone to blame or perhaps there is some rationalization to help justify the feeling. There are a lot of people getting laid off. The economy is in the tank. The company that let you go is evil. These are all excuses I have heard over the years but none of these thoughts help. Any thought directed by the ego is not in your best interest. It simply manifests into your perceived reality. Choose the other option, the option to go with Spirit. Consider yourself on an adventure. Let it be. Use this time to still your mind, evaluate your situation objectively and let go of any negative thought, doubt or resistance in your mind. Take inventory of your competencies and skills and give thanks for the many blessings you have in the present moment. Channel any stress or doubt you feel into sacred intentions and positive actions, steps you can take immediately to reemploy yourself, sell any unnecessary items or perhaps even move locations. Embrace the adventure you are in rather than resist it. We learn much about our true Self in circumstances like this and it is our response that makes all the difference.

Question: My wife of many years recently announced that she wants a divorce. I really struggle 'letting be' moments like this. How can I let this be?

When faced with a difficult task, it helps to have a useful tool. Use the Ring of Peace to help you handle this situation with grace. Let it also remind you that you are not alone. You are never alone. You have spiritual support at your side throughout every moment of every day. Learn to trust the Holy Spirit as He guides you through this difficult time. Begin with let be. Seek to understand the current situation. What are you feeling? What is your wife feeling? What thoughts are you both holding in mind? To what extent is there fear involved? Keep in mind that fear exists in the absence of unconditional love. If you do not love each other without condition, then you are both accepting fear into your consciousness. You are accepting the ego's interpretation of things: fear, judgment, lust, jealously, control, criticism, doubt, abandonment, betrayal, humiliation and suffering. Recognize at the Let Be phase that you cannot change your wife. You can only change your own mind about your wife, divorce or otherwise. Accept who she is and acknowledge that you are both the light of God, deeply connected whether you are married or not. Deep within you abides the capacity to overlook, to forgive without condemnation and to free yourself from a human relationship that may not be a good fit at this time. Chances are, you will uncover a host of thoughts that you hold in mind, fueled by fear, that manifest into very painful feelings. These are the thoughts you need to release. In addition, let go of your fear by committing to loving your wife unconditionally, no matter what. You have the capacity to do this. You just need to overcome your own judgments and doubts—doubts you may harbor about your future, your children, material things, possessions, settlements, misperceptions, rumors, accusations, social standing or humiliation. Surrender these mental attachments to God through the Holy Spirit. You do not need them. With a shift in emotion, from fear to love, you will see your wife in a different light. She may still want a divorce, but you now see her, yourself and the situation very differently. You are at peace with it, despite the outcome. It may be helpful to note that as you release any attachment or clinging you hold in mind, you release patterns of behavior, thoughts and tendencies that limit you. This might translate into manifesting the most exciting future imaginable—something you do not know at this time. The divorce, on a deeper level, may be just the karmic lesson you signed up for with your wife—soul to soul—in a distant past on a different plain to advance both of you. Now you just need to get on with it. Your marriage meant something, no doubt. Your divorce will mean something, too. No doubt. Let be. Let go. Let see. Let flow.

Question: I am still angry about the way my grandmother suffered through her remaining days on earth. I am angry at the healthcare system, the absence of good, long-term care and the government for cutting funding. How can I apply the Ring of Peace to my situation? I intend to challenge the healthcare system.

There is no need for anger. Your grandmother is not angry. She is at peace. Why should you be angry? Do not add to your Grandma's karmic debt by allowing her situation to cause you pain and unrest. She does not want this for you and you need not dictate what she wants. Let your grandmother be at peace. Let yourself be at peace. Let go of your perception and judgment of the situation and do not *mind* your ego interpretation of things. Embrace the Truth. All is as it should be for our spiritual development. Let go of hatred. Let go of shame. Let go of guilt.

Let go of rage. Let go of pride. Pursue your work with love. Do something positive for your grandmother out of love and joy, not hostility and revenge. Demonstrate your love for her by moving forward with compassion and forgiveness. Put your heart into your pursuits, not your sword. Heal yourself first by changing your mind about the situation and then concentrate on changing the healthcare system. You will have far greater effect with love.

Question: Can you comment more on karma? I seem to run into one problem after another. Am I destined to suffer in life because of bad debt?

You are not destined to suffer in life. This is not your reason for being here. However, to transcend suffering, which does exist, you must release the cause to this suffering. As the Buddha said, there is a way out of suffering (Nirvana) and you hold the key. Karma is an ancient term meaning memory, or cause and effect. It also translates into work profession or duty. Our karma is an energy imprint we carry with us as we go through life. What some people call 'good karma' translates into prosperity, good fortune and well-being. Everything just seems to fall into place. It is as if we are owed positive outcomes from positive actions in the past, helping the world in some way. On the other hand, 'bad karma' translates into tough luck, frequent demise and a life of hard work. This may mean we carry with us a profession or duty to serve in some way—a means to paying off our karmic debt. Either way, we can cleanse ourselves from any karmic debt by spiritually altering our thought system and corresponding behavior. This can be done in a number of ways, including meditation, chanting healing mantras and applying the Ring of Peace. To free ourselves of karmic debt, we need a means to let go of negative energies, alter our perceptions and flow with the will of God. Learn and practice these techniques and you can free yourself of your current karma.

Question: I really struggle being in the now. The nature of my work is to plan ahead and be prepared. How do I use the Ring of Peace with such a demanding schedule?

The nature of your work is to be in the eternal now—always. There is no time but the present. It is in the present that we plan ahead and it is in the present that we prepare ourselves. It is always in the present that we do whatever it is we do. To perform most effectively, we need a focused mind, an ability to remain conscious, alert and aware in the present moment. It is when the mind drifts into the past or the future that we lose focus, miss opportunities and make mistakes. Even when we visualize a future state, a key characteristic among effective change agents, we do it in the now. We paint a clear and compelling picture of the future as if it exists now. We sense it. We feel it. We see in the mind's eye. We experience it as if it is happening here and now. This translates into a heightened sense of awareness, a keen advantage to manifesting positive change. Practice the Ring of Peace to elevate your awareness. Use it to see with greater clarity and understanding by releasing clouded judgment. Use it to set priorities and discern meaningful work from meaningless tasks. These are the characteristics that matter most in the workplace, especially when facing a demanding schedule.

Question: How many cycles of the Ring of Peace do I need to go through before I feel any difference?

While patience is a virtue and it is probable that you will need practice, you should feel a difference with one cycle. There is only one way to find out. Try it. Commit to it. Choose a problem or a conflict you are trying to solve right now and apply the tool. Keep in mind you are the user of the tool so it is your application that matters most. Think of the ring like it is a set of golf clubs. You can study the clubs. You can intellectualize the game of golf. You can learn all of the rules and you can watch the pros play golf on television. But you do not know golf until you go out and start swinging the clubs for yourself, even if it is a bit humbling. You will not know the Ring of Peace until you start using it.

Question: What happens when someone falls off the wagon? I have been seeking spiritual awareness for several years now, but I still have a tendency to get trapped by my ego. I know it is my ego fighting back and afterwards I feel bad about it. What can I do?

Get back on the wagon. Take a Mulligan (another shot). You are experiencing common, predictable trials. With each trial, you are being given a chance to choose wisely and to learn from your choice. Ask yourself "Am I listening to the ego, or am I listening to the voice for God, the Holy Spirit within me?" Just knowing the difference is a huge step in a positive direction, an elevation of consciousness. Sometimes a seeker lapses into ego judgment, choosing temptations of the body. This is human. Just remember that the human body is for communion. It is for helping people, forgiving one another and reuniting as one. It is for pulling together, not dividing and isolating one another as separate beings. This challenges us to go beyond seeing physical form with the human eye. To fulfill our function, we must develop spiritual vision, allowing us to see the oneness we all share, the glorious field of consciousness itself. There are many different ways to enlighten the mind and foster communion among people but they all start with this awareness, this constancy of purpose. When we lose sight of our true purpose, we risk falling back into habitual ego behaviors. This leads to feelings of guilt and shame, a perfect opportunity to reapply the Ring of Peace. Consider your wagon ride an on-going practice, a series of continuous trials, not a one-time event. You already know about the temptations and traps of the ego, a sure sign of your spiritual awareness. Now continue your ascension with conscious discipline and practice. Seek and ye shall find.

Question: What should I do if I do not feel any different after going through the cycle?

Try again, but this time let go of any agenda or attachment you might hold in mind, consciously or subconsciously. Remember that the Ring of Peace is not about 'adding' anything new to our lives—love, joy, peace, enlightenment. These attributes exist in us now. It is about helping us remove the hidden constraints and limiting beliefs that restrict these innate characteristics from shining through. If we attempt to apply the Ring of Peace with any preconceived solution or desire, we are demonstrating distrust in God and in the tool. We are trying to force an answer, probably a solution that appeals to the ego. This will short-circuit the process. It is the equivalent of praying *for* something specific, a type of prayer that usually leads to perceived defeat (i.e. I did not get what I prayed for). The Holy Spirit answers all prayers at all times. The difference is that His answers are not what the ego specifies in the prayers. The Holy Spirit does not recognize ego. He only answers prayers with a response that is spiritually best for the common good, a solution that heals at a deeper level, soul to soul. When you use the Ring of Peace, keep this in mind. Surrender any ego agenda to God and allow the ring to clear your mind and your life of all clutter. Trust that your true will, in alignment with God's will, is being done. This is the language of the Holy Spirit.

Question: Are there any risks associated with the Ring of Peace?

It is always the ego that asks about risk. Spirit knows no danger. From an ego perspective, there are all kinds of risks associated with finding inner peace. What will the ego say and do if we do not listen to it anymore? What will happen to all of our doubt, all of our drama and all of our dissatisfaction? Will this be the end of the ego, the end of conflict, the end of suffering? Will this be the second coming of Christ, an arrival we all hold deep within us? How terrifying might this be to an ego that lives in a perpetual state of fear to begin with? The answer is very terrifying! This is why the ego will put up such a fight. It will not accept your decision quietly. It will sense something is 'wrong' and try to convince you to give up, to abandon your pursuit of peace and enlightenment. Do not go on this journey, it will say. It is dangerous. It will cost you this and you will have to sacrifice that. Your spiritual pursuit carries with it enormous risk from an ego perspective, a journey that leaves the ego behind. From a spiritual perspective, there is no risk at all. You can enjoy all that you have now and so much more, beyond doubt.

Question: What is the true meaning of love?

The true meaning of love cannot be taught. It can only be experienced. It is the one true emotion we all carry within us but we must *feel* it for ourselves to know it. It is what we are made of. Without love, we cannot exist, we cannot breathe and we cannot know God. Love is the glue that holds the universe together. It is the life force, the spiritual bond that unites us as one. It is from love that we were created and it is with love that we exist now. True love is without condition. God does not set limitations on His love for us. He loves us no matter what, always. We are the prodigal sons and no matter what we do, He welcomes us home. The ego interpretation of love is quite different. With the ego, we see and hear limitations and conditions being placed on love. These 'strings attached' range from Hollywood romance and drama to marital contracts and requirements. The ego's misperception of love leaves people feeling confused and subconsciously afraid. Lust and desire are substituted for love, and deals are made offering one in return for the other. Conditional love is given and then taken away in marriages and divorces, intimate partnerships that break down and friendships that form and then dissolve. The ego leads us to believe that love can be used to barter, to trade and to take away. True love has no opposite and cannot be taken away. It is timeless and omnipresent, just as God is. We do not fall in and out of true love. Instead, we are either aware of it (enlightened) or we are not (asleep). When the Buddha awakened, this is the love he felt, the true love of God. Jesus saw the same love in all people, the love of Christ. We have this potential to wake up and experience true, unconditional love. We can see and flow with the love of God when we let go of the blinders, filters and conditions we are programmed to use. Enlightenment is about embracing our true nature and cleansing ourselves of the harmful subconscious 'programs,' misperceptions and mental viruses dictated by the ego.

Questions: Can you comment on evil, Satan and hell? Are these things real? I believe that Satan has had a lot to do with my misfortunes in the past.

Your opinions and beliefs manifest into your perceived reality even if they are not true. In this case, if you believe in evil, Satan and hell, you will experience it. Your ego mind will search for and find evidence to convince you that it is right. Evil will present itself to you every day. You will see it on the news. You will hear about it at work. You will witness it on the street corner. Satan will cause car accidents, natural disasters and deadly diseases. People will suffer for their sins. Hell will present itself as an option every day, triggering more fear and self-doubt. The ego thrives on this drama because it provides perfect cover for a mad idea. True reality is of God. It is positive, permanent, loving and abundant. It is what always has been and it is what always will be. It is what we *have* by giving away. Love is real. Joy is real. Peace is real. Forgiveness is real. Spirit is real. The atonement is real. Heaven is real. Anything that does not meet these divine conditions is not real, including the ego and its misinterpretations about anything. As a result, evil, Satan and hell are not real even though the ego thinks otherwise. They are illusions of the ego mind, perceptions intended to threaten and harm us. They exist only in the absence of love. Think about this. Would a truly loving God wish His children harm? Would a truly loving God condemn or punish His children? Would a truly loving God not give His children another chance to atone for mistakes? Release the ego and its doubts about God and free yourself from any and all perception about evil, Satan and hell. Look on the world with love and you will see it differently. This is how we transcend our karma. There are indeed many people making ignorant mistakes, but deep within all of us abides the light of God. Offer peace and forgiveness and it is yours in return.

Question: What is the true meaning of forgiveness?

True forgiveness means overlooking mistakes as if they never happened. It is a process of letting be and letting go and letting see and letting flow. It means holding no grudges or hard feelings toward anyone or anything. It is a gateway to inner peace. It is trusting in God and the perfect harmony and balance of the universe. Take a moment now to consider a time in your life when you felt betrayed, hurt, violated or humiliated. Do you still hold these thoughts and feelings? What good is this doing you? Let go of your ego thoughts and seek Truth. Recognize that being vengeful or condemning toward others does no good at all. It is a trap, set by the ego. True forgiveness means freeing yourself from this trap and seeing the world through the eyes of Spirit. It means recognizing the spiritual nature of all humankind and co-creating with God a life of inner peace.

Question: How do I find my true purpose in life?

We all share the same purpose. We just use different means to realize it. Our united purpose is to return home to God, to heaven. Because we are of God, He awaits our return. We belong together. For most people, this 'awakening' can take a long time, many lifetimes in fact. We reincarnate and try again (with different karmas) until we learn to wake up and transcend the karmic debts we carry with us. Thus, over many millennia the human race has been spiritually evolving, elevating to higher levels of collective consciousness. The spiritual masters have shown us the way, but the ego has put forth strong resistance. Whatever it is you do for a living, recognize the spiritual light you carry within you. Use it to light the way for others. Approach your work with love and compassion. Release all fear and doubt. Do what you do for the greater common good, not just for yourself. Consider the context of your work and not just the content. Stop and ask yourself from time to time, how does my work bring joy and peace to people in need? What problems am I solving with my efforts? How is the world a better place because of what I am doing? You will know you are serving your purpose in life when you *feel* it deep within you, when you combine positive thoughts and intentions with the emotion of love. It doesn't matter if you are teaching classes, driving bulldozers or mowing lawns. Spirit will shine through when you align your will with God's.

Question: When I feel myself becoming sad or depressed, what can I do besides calling a doctor or taking a prescription?

Many people around the world are now 'programmed' to call doctors and ask for medicines to fix an ailment. Rather than research and apply healthy alternatives that address root causes, they rely instead on temporary solutions that relieve symptoms, often with serious side effects. To compound the problem, many doctors are currently trained only in traditional practices without knowledge of natural alternatives and prevention techniques. This translates into many unnecessary surgeries and prescriptions, often at a very high cost with very high risk. It is wise to learn about alternatives, especially natural healing supplements and spiritual techniques. Begin with the mind, the source of all stress and disease. Depression is not your natural state. Use the Ring of Peace to uncover any negative or depressing thoughts you hold in mind. What are these thoughts and why do you accept them? Write them down and then throw them away. What makes you feel sad? What is your karma? What is your consciousness? Why do you accept these thoughts? Learn to replace these negative ego thoughts with healthy alternatives. Seek to remember who you truly are, a perfect extension of God. Use positive daily affirmations to reprogram your thought system. Learn meditation techniques to release any unconscious guilt or shame you hold in mind. Research and choose natural health supplements to help bring your body chemistry back into balance as you cleanse your mind. You can choose from many all natural 'nutriceuticals' appearing on the market each year, backed by credible, conscientious medical and scientific study and without negative side effects. Look for these, but do not expect your doctor to know about them. Help your doctor help you. Alternative, natural healing practices have not been included in traditional medical training. Consider starting or changing your exercise routine. Try something new like yoga, swimming or walking along nature trails. Most importantly, recognize that your true Self, your inner Spirit, is never sad or depressed. It is only your ego making you feel this way. Your true nature is that of joy and unbridled enthusiasm. You just have layers of mental clutter and anguish to let go of to recognize and unleash your undaunted, perfectly whole Spirit. No doctor or pill on the planet can do this for you. True healing always begins in the mind.

Question: I am not happy about the shape of my body. Can you help?

You can help yourself. Start by being happy with your body, in whatever shape it is in. Let it be, without judgment. Your constant criticism and resistance is only making your situation worse. Think about all the things you really do like about your body—perhaps your eyes or hair color or the fact that you have all of your fingers and toes. Thank God for the body you have. Next, begin to assess the leadership of your body—your mind. What are you telling your body on a day to day basis, consciously and subconsciously? Are you loving and kind? Are you supportive and encouraging? Are you positive and optimistic? Are you disciplined and forgiving? Begin to surface two or three 'inputs' you can change quickly or let go of that will lead to better 'outputs.' Seek ways to build momentum. Consider any tendencies you have that affect your body. It really doesn't take much to surface several things you can change to improve your condition. Your best, most sustainable solutions will be actions you can take immediately that are easy and enjoyable. Avoid solutions that carry a high risk of abandonment at first. For example, if you do not like running or lifting weights, find an alternative you do like. Try bicycling or walking in the park. If you like eating or drinking something that is not healthy for you, replace it with something you like that is healthy for you. You will be most successful with solutions that come from within you, not from outside of you. Your body is neutral. It responds to your mind. Change your mind and your body will follow.

Question: I would like to apply what you are teaching, but I am just too busy to keep up with all the information and advice on how to improve my life. How do I get off the treadmill?

Push the stop button before you find yourself in crisis. Stop making excuses as to why you cannot do it now. This tendency to procrastinate important choices, and the thought system that governs it, does not change of its own accord. It remains fixed, holding you captive, running on automatic. You will remain on the treadmill indefinitely, losing steam as you go. Take responsibility now for changing this. What I am teaching does not take much time to apply. In most cases, it is an 'in place of' strategy as opposed to an 'in addition to' strategy. This means that it does not require any more time in a day. It just requires an exchange of activities. For example, if you wanted to start your day with a meditative cleansing of mind, you could set your alarm twenty minutes earlier and be finished with this exercise by breakfast. That is all it takes to apply the technique. Replace twenty minutes of sleep with twenty minutes of meditation. You might also find opportunities on the way to and from work to 'keep up with some of the information and advice' available. I have mentioned that books and CDs are excellent resources. Contemplation is another form of application that is easy to apply and requires very little time. Choose a mantra or affirmation to use throughout each day to reprogram your mind. Write your affirmation down on a piece of paper and keep it in your pocket or in a visible place. Repeat it at least once every hour and contemplate its meaning. Look for ways to apply the affirmation immediately, throughout the day. You can also join users groups, associations and organizations dedicated to increasing awareness and elevating human consciousness. Many of these groups offer books, seminars, retreats, videos, conferencing, online support services and research. You only have to express your sacred intent, prioritize your activities and exercise your will. There is more than enough time in the day to accomplish everything that is truly important. We all have the same amount of time in a day. Setting priorities and executing our will makes the difference.

Question: By most standards, I am very successful in life. I am healthy, happily married with wonderful children, financially secure and living my life according to my plan. I was blessed with loving parents, excellent schooling and a very positive upbringing. Despite all this, I still feel like something is missing. I still have doubts. I do not feel whole and complete. Deep down, I suppose I fear losing something. Can you help?

You speak volumes. Whenever a person is attached to an outcome, any outcome, there is an element of fear. Many people recognize this as risk—the risk of getting married, the risk of having children, the risk of losing something of perceived value. Some go so far as to *not* commit to anyone or anything for fear of pain or loss. The key here is not to avoid or abandon relationships or the pursuit of happiness. In fact, it is just the opposite, as you have done. Spirit seeks loving relationships and meaningful communion. It is where we all came from and it is where we are meant to be. The difference is in *letting go* of attachments and aversions. Let be and let go. Trust in God and 'the Way.' Surrender your worries and doubts to the Holy Spirit. They do you and your family no good. This does not mean literally selling your house and car or abandoning what you have worked hard to achieve. It simply means letting go of the attachments you hold in mind, bringing you to a state of 'not mindingness.' In this state of being, you no longer associate yourself with your wife, your car, your house, your job title, your children, your watch, your clothes or your bank account. You are simply at peace, with or without these attachments. This is the let see and let flow state of mind after repeated applications of the Ring of Peace. At this level, you find that you actually love your wife and children more deeply than ever before, but without fear or worry. This is unconditional love, no strings attached, good or bad. You find that you actually love your job, your house and your achievements more deeply than ever before, but without any anxiety or stress. You reach a state of mind where you feel spiritually free, without any fear or doubt about anything. You could lose your family, your house, your job, your car, your savings—anything you have held up as value—and you know you will come out of it just fine. You begin to realize that you are not defined by any of these temporary things. You are defined by God and you are forever protected, never alone. In this state of being, you realize that you are surrounded by infinite opportunities to extend your peace to others and share your lessons learned.

Question: You often make reference to A Course in Miracles. What is this course and why should I believe it?

A Course in Miracles is three documents: a Text (31 chapter narration of spiritual answers), a Workbook (365 lessons, one for each day of the year) and a Teacher's Manual. The *Course* was first published in 1975 by The Foundation for Inner Peace, a non-profit organization. This publication captures over seven years of 'channeling' and note-taking by Helen Schucman, Ph.D., a research psychologist at Columbia University's College of Physicians and Surgeons. Helen was supported and assisted during this 'startling' time in her life by her trusted colleague, Bill Thetford, Ph.D., head of the department. This was a challenging time for Helen because the 'Voice' she kept hearing was quite insistent that she write down what it was saying. Helen was skeptical at first—downright fearful in fact—and Bill offered her sympathy, understanding and counsel. They were both agnostic in belief at the time and quite surprised by the words the Voice was sharing. Being trained to work with rational scientific methods and principles, not mystical ways, they were initially very concerned about their careers and reputations. It was the wisdom in the *words* and the life improvements that followed that kept them going.

Today, *A Course in Miracles* is widely considered to be a direct channeling from Jesus, despite the many skeptics who are troubled by this. It does not matter if you are skeptical or not. The only thing that matters is your own experience with the words, the exercises and your results. To many people, including myself, the *Course* is one of the clearest, most profound spiritual documents ever published. It is truly life-changing, whether you initially believe it or not. It is not affiliated or connected with any religion and it does not claim exclusivity on Truth or the path to atonement and salvation. It simply gives us a choice to accelerate our spiritual growth, joy and inner peace by removing obstacles and listening to our own inner teacher. The same holds true for the Ring of Peace. This is our choice, our timing. God bless.

A Blessing to Contemplate

By the grace of God, I have the wisdom and patience to let be:
    Let be the beauty of the eternal now
    Let be the joy of life
    Let be the will of God

By the grace of God, I have the courage and strength to let go:
    Let go the grief of past
    Let go the anxiety of future
    Let go the fear and doubt of ego

By the grace of God, I have the will and capacity to let see:
    Let see the lessons learned
    Let see the light of God in others
    Let see the oneness of Christ

By the grace of God, I have the love and compassion to let flow.
Let flow equanimity and abundance with ease
Let flow the perfect harmony of life
Let flow the Spirit of God

By the light of God, I am healed

By the light of God, we are all healed

'Isn't it amazing how fast we learn when we have nothing to fear?'—JJM

Get Published, Inc!
Thorofare, NJ 08086
18 November 2009
BA2009261